An Athlete's Guide to Agents

An Athlete's Guide to Agents

Robert H. Ruxin

Indiana University Press • Bloomington

First Midland Book Edition 1983

Copyright © 1982 by Robert H. Ruxin
All rights reserved

No part of this book may be reproduced or utilized in any form or by any means, electronic or mechanical, including photocopying and recording, or by any information storage and retrieval system, without permission in writing from the publisher. The Association of American University Presses' Resolution on Permissions constitutes the only exception to this prohibition.

Manufactured in the United States of America

Library of Congress Cataloging in Publication Data

Ruxin, Robert H.
    An athlete's guide to agents.

    Bibliography: p.
    1. Sports agents. I. Title.
GV734.5.R88   1982   796'.024796   82-47781
ISBN 0-253-10400-9
ISBN 0-253-20290-6 (pbk.)
1 2 3 4 5 87 86 85 84 83

CONTENTS

Foreword by Wiles Hallock	vii
Preface	ix
Introduction	3
Special Warning: The Student-Athlete and Professional Sports	7

I: Agents—What, Why, and for Whom — 11

Question 1: What is an agent?	13
Question 2: Why agents now?	14
Question 3: What can an agent do for me?	17
Question 4: How does someone qualify to be an agent?	21
Question 5: Should I represent myself?	25
Question 6: What other professional advice do I need?	28

II: Matchmaking—Athlete Meets Agent — 33

Question 7: How do I find an agent?	35
Question 8: How do I choose an agent?	39
Question 9: What if I'm thinking about turning pro early?	43
Question 10: How does signing a power of attorney affect the athlete-agent relationship?	47
Question 11: Do I need a written agreement?	49

III: Paying the Agent — 53

Question 12: How much will it cost me?	55
Question 13: When do I pay?	57
Question 14: Should the agent collect his fee directly from the club?	59

IV: Conflict—The Agent's Other Interests — 61

Question 15: How might a club influence my relationship with my agent?	63

Question 16: How can the agent's other clients
 affect my interests? 67
Question 17: What does disclosure do for me? 71

V: The Agent and His Principles 75

Question 18: What if I want to renegotiate my contract? 77

VI: Regulation 87

Question 19: Who regulates agents? 89
Question 20: What role do players' associations play? 93

Conclusion: The Athlete's Responsibility 99

Glossary 101

Appendixes 105

   A. The Professional Drafts 105

   B. Salary Information 112

   C. Sample Contracts 117
      Athlete–Agent 117
      Athlete–Investment Manager 120
      Athlete–Financial Manager 123

   D. Uniform Players' Contracts 127
      Baseball: National League 127
      National Football League 137

   E. Agent Authorization Form 144

   F. California Statute Regulating Agents 148

   G. Directory 156

Sources 159

Foreword

With the increasing exploitation of prospective professional athletes at the high school and college levels by unscrupulous or incompetent agents, it has become painfully evident that these young people need accurate information to assist them in making intelligent and thoughtful decisions during the difficult transition from school or college to professional sports. In response to this need for information, the National Collegiate Athletic Association (NCAA) provided a generous grant to the Collegiate Commissioners Association (CCA) to address this problem. The NCAA Pro Sports Liaison Committee, staffed by Tom Hansen and Steve Morgan, working closely with the CCA, determined that the most effective way to reach college athletes would be a two-pronged approach—through wide distribution of a free CCA pamphlet sensitizing student-athletes to the need to prepare themselves for the business aspects of becoming professional athletes, and through endorsement of this book, *An Athlete's Guide to Agents*, which should be in every sports library.

An Athlete's Guide to Agents expands and elaborates upon the issues and warnings raised in the CCA pamphlet and contains specific, detailed, sound, and practical advice for both the student-athlete and the professional sports participant. Its author, attorney Robert Ruxin, has provided a readily understandable and fascinating guide through the maze of financial pitfalls and legal decisions facing the career professional athlete. Ruxin, whose interest in the complexities of player-agent relationships goes back to law school days at Harvard where he prepared a paper on the subject, has consulted college coaches, institutional and conference athletic administrators and faculty representatives, pro sports league executives, team representatives, player association officials, professional athletes, agent organization personnel, and agents.

Important cooperation has also come from Indiana University's Center for Law and Sports and from the Big Ten Conference through Commissioner Wayne Duke. Ruxin has drawn significantly from the work of Mike Slive, former Assistant Director of the Pac-10 Conference and now Director of Athletics at Cornell University.

As chairman of the Professional Sports Liaison Committee, I commend Bob Ruxin's work and, along with fellow committee member Carl James, speaking on behalf of the Collegiate Commissioners Association, strongly recommend *An Athlete's Guide to Agents* to all athletes with professional aspirations and to their coaches, advisors, and families. It is clearly and interestingly written, provides specific examples of athlete-agent relationships, and contains copies of useful documents and procedures, including sample contracts applicable to professional sports. It accurately reflects the current NCAA rules relating to collegiate eligibility and professional sports. It may not please the predatory or self-serving agent, but for the legitimate and ethical agent this book can serve as a valuable addition to his or her body of knowledge.

Wiles Hallock
Executive Director
Pacific-10 Conference

Preface

Although this book evolved from a paper prepared for the Harvard Law School independent writing program, it is written as a handbook for athletes. I have avoided cumbersome footnotes to make the book more easily readable. Much of the information comes from interviews and correspondence with agents or persons involved with agents and from meetings of agents and sports lawyers. Quotations from newspapers or magazines are identified in the text with attribution to the publication. All significant sources are listed in the back of the book.

In addition to providing an overall introduction to the sports agent business, the book is organized to allow easy access to information about a particular topic. For instance, an athlete concerned about how much and when to pay his agent can turn to the section entitled "Paying the Agent." The appendixes provide supplementary information on topics ranging from how the draft process works in each professional sport to the text of the California law regulating sports agents. Thus the book is both a handbook and a reference tool.

I am grateful to the many people involved with professional and college sports as agents, attorneys, players, coaches, administrators, union staff, and league staff who took the time to be interviewed for the book or to critique the drafts. Several law professors were instrumental in the development of the project and in bringing it to publication: Roger Fisher of Harvard, who, as my adviser, suggested that I write a paper about agents aimed at the consumer; John Weistart of Duke, author of the seminal treatise *The Law of Sports*; and Ron Waicukauski, Director of the Center for Law and Sports at Indiana University, who invited me to deliver a paper on college athletes and agents at a conference on Amateur Sports and the Law. Other professors who offered assistance were Roy Shapiro of the Harvard Business School and David Keuchle of the Harvard Graduate School of Education, who advised me on a case study of Luis Tiant's contract problems with the Boston Red Sox; and Robert Berry of Boston College Law

School and Glenn Wong of the University of Massachusetts Sports Management Program. Wiles Hallock, chairman of the NCAA Professional Sports Liaison Committee, committee members Carl James, Bob Moorman, Ernie Casale, Ruth Alexander, and Mary Roby, and Tom Hansen and Steve Morgan of the NCAA staff provided guidance, access to college and professional sports officials, and support.

I with to thank the attorneys and staff in the Washington, D.C., and Seattle offices of my law firm, Preston, Thorgrimson, Ellis & Holman, for their assistance. Peggy Shukur provided invaluable editorial help. Most important, I appreciate the persistent encouragement from my parents, Arnold and Sherle Ruxin, and my sister, Suzanne Ruxin Fishkin. This book is dedicated to them.

An Athlete's Guide to Agents

Andy Messersmith has changed agents and now expects to find a new career with the Yankees. It used to be that a ballplayer would get his domestic life straightened out to make a fresh start. Now it's changing agents.

—Dick Young, *The Sporting News*,
January 21, 1978

Surely, the growing power of sports agents was never more graphically shown than during the ceremonies. Pitcher Frank Tanana's best man was his agent. . . .

—Dick Miller, *The Sporting News*,
February 4, 1978

Sorkin Tells State Crime Unit
Sports Agents Duped Clients

—Headline, *The New York Times*,
February 2, 1978

Agents are at fault—McGuire

—Headline, *Chicago Tribune*,
October 13, 1980

Are Agents Pack of Parasites?
Some Gouge, Lie and Cheat Clients;
Others Do Honest, Competent Job

—Headline, *The Sporting News*,
February 6, 1982

Introduction

The sports agent has become essential to most athletes' wellbeing. A good agent can help a professional athlete attain financial and mental stability during and after his career. An incompetent or dishonest agent can ruin an athlete's playing career and threaten his financial security for years afterward. He can also jeopardize an undergraduate athlete's collegiate eligibility and cause the athlete's university to forfeit athletic contests and television revenue.

As former Marquette basketball coach Al McGuire observed at a recent sports medicine seminar, "A lot of problems in pro sports today are with the agents. It's a lot like a bouncer in a bar. If there's not a fight, the bouncer will create one and throw somebody out. It seems like athletes find an agent and all of a sudden they get into a turmoil type of thing."

Stories about agents who take advantage of their clients are too common. Two basketball players on the same NBA team who were represented by the same agent began to compare notes on the agent. Each decided to terminate the agent's services. But their phone calls were not answered; they sent a registered letter: no response. Finally, they flew to the agent's city, tracked him down, and led him to the bank to get their money back. They were lucky; the agent still held their funds.

Another basketball player, a seven-year NBA veteran, wasn't so fortunate. Known as a penny pincher, he was razzed by his teammates about the old car he drove. When he decided to buy a new car, he called his agent. His money was gone.

Consider the plight of then 25-year-old Dennis Duval, an all-American basketball player at Syracuse University and briefly a guard with two NBA teams. "I'm the victim of a crime and I'm being asked to pay for it," Duval told a federal court as he filed for bankruptcy. His agent, Richard Sorkin, handled his money and supposedly paid his bills, Duval said. But Duval allegedly lost $30,000 to Sorkin, who was sentenced to three years in prison for having lost an estimated $1.2 million belonging to twenty athletes.

One major newspaper, *Newsday* of Long Island, concluded after a lengthy investigation that the world of sports agency was "teeming with the contemptible." Among the examples cited by *Newsday* were:

- an offer by a New York agent to Dean Smith, North Carolina basketball coach, of 2.5 percent of a player's contract if Smith helped him sign the player;
- a football player who signed agreements with five agents before the player or any of the agents began negotiations with the Los Angeles Rams;
- an agent whose total bills for three years equaled one year of his client's three-year contract;
- an NBA guard who stated in a sworn deposition that his agent told him that he (the agent) was afraid of going to jail for falsifying federal income tax returns;
- football and basketball agents who are willing to sell out their players for under-the-table payments from pro teams.

A professional athlete can protect himself from the disreputable agents by carefully choosing an agent and working closely with him. This book is aimed at the consumer—the athlete—and his family and personal advisers, as well as prospective agents, sports executives, high school and college coaches and athletic directors, and those concerned with regulating the industry. After reading this guide an athlete will be better prepared to question intelligently his agent or those who seek to represent him. For the serious sports fan, the book offers some insight into why, as *Newsweek* stated on the eve of the 1982 football strike, agents and lawyers "seem to enjoy a disproportionate power on the modern [sports] scene."

This is not a shopping guide to individual agents. It is not intended to pass judgment on any particular agent. In essence this is a warning label outside the package of useful services an agent will try to sell to an athlete. While it will alert the athlete to the potential dangers of associating with a dishonest, incompetent, or unscrupulous agent, it will also instruct the athlete on how to maximize the benefits a good agent offers.

SPECIAL WARNING:
The Student-Athlete and Professional Sports

Jeff Ruland spent what would have been his senior year at Iona College playing basketball in Europe. Ruland didn't choose to leave school. He had no choice after it became known that he had violated NCAA rules by signing with an agent prior to his junior year and by accepting cash and other favors. Ruland retained an attorney to untangle the legal problems relating to the agent and hired a new agent to negotiate with the Washington Bullets.

The Bullets felt they had Ruland over a barrel, according to his agent's firm. The contract offered was not as good as the agent thought it should be. Furthermore, since the Bullets had Wes Unseld and Elvin Hayes, it appeared that Ruland might receive a lot of bench time. The agent recommended that Ruland play in Europe and secured a job for him with a basketball team in Barcelona, Spain.

A year later, while preparing for what became an outstanding rookie season as a Washington Bullet center, Ruland offered some advice to college athletes concerning agents. "Don't talk to any of them," he said during a radio interview. "Too many agents are out there for themselves."

Ruland publicly conceded that what he did was wrong and noted that many other college athletes did the same thing. But the knowledge that others did the same thing didn't restore Jeff Ruland's eligibility; it could not bring back his senior year. And had Ruland played his senior year at Iona, he probably would have signed a more lucrative NBA contract.

Special Warning

Because campuses are crawling with agents and would-be agents eager to sign college athletes regardless of what the NCAA rules allow, it is vitally important that every coach, student-athlete, athlete's family, and all personal advisors to athletes understand what the NCAA forbids and what it allows in regard to contacts with professional sports agents and teams.* Even if many infractions go undetected, and even if some of the rules seem to be not always in the athlete's best interest, a student-athlete who violates NCAA rules may find himself in a situation like Jeff Ruland's.

NCAA Rules:

Forbid an athlete to agree, either orally or in writing, to be represented by an agent or organization in the marketing of his athletic ability or reputation until after completion of his last intercollegiate contest, *including* postseason games. This prohibition includes entering an agreement which is "not effective" until after the last game;

Forbid an athlete or any representative of the athlete to *negotiate* or *sign* a playing contract in any sport in which he intends to compete, or to market the name or image of the athlete; it makes no difference whether or not the contract is legally enforceable;

Forbid an athlete to ask to be placed on a professional league's draft list, whether or not he withdraws his name before the draft, whether or not he is actually drafted, and whether or not he signs a professional contract. This rule primarily affects undergraduate basketball players who apply for the NBA draft;†

---

*The NCAA rules governing amateurism and the relationships between college athletes and professional sports agents are set forth in the manual of the National Collegiate Athletic Association. This book is revised annually in March.
†For a description of the draft process in each professional sport, see Appendix A.

Special Warning

Forbid an athlete to accept expenses or gifts of any kind (including meals and transportation) from an agent (or anyone else) who wishes to provide service to the athlete; such payment is not allowed, because it would be compensation based on athletic skills and a preferential benefit not available to other students;

Forbid an athlete to receive preferential benefits or treatment (for example, loans with deferred pay-back) bestowed on the athlete because of his reputation, skill, or payback potential as a professional athlete;

Forbid an athlete to retain professional services for personal reasons at less than the normal charge from a representative of his school's athletic interests;

Forbid a coach or other member of the athletic staff to represent directly or indirectly a student-athlete in the marketing of his athletic ability or reputation to a professional sports team or organization, and to receive any compensation or gratuities for such activity.

NCAA Rules:

Allow an athlete to compete professionally in sports in which he does not participate for the university (but signing a professional contract terminates his eligibility for an athletic scholarship in any sport);

Allow an athlete to retain an agent specifically limited in *writing* to representing him in those sports in which he competes as a professional;

Allow an athlete to retain an attorney for matters of a personal nature, including evaluating the terms of a proposed professional contract, providing the attorney does not represent the athlete in negotiating such a contract and providing the student-athlete pays normal fees;

Allow an athlete to talk to an agent, providing he neither agrees to be represented by nor accepts *anything* of any value from the agent;

Allow an athlete to ask a pro league or team about his eligibility to be drafted.

The impact of these rules concerning agreements with agents and accepting favors from agents will be examined in Part II, "Athlete Meets Agent."

I
Agents—What, Why, and for Whom

Question 1: What is an agent?
Question 2: Why agents now?
Question 3: What can an agent do for me?
Question 4: How does someone qualify to be an agent?
Question 5: Should I represent myself?
Question 6: What other professional advice do I need?

Question 1: What is an agent?

The term "agent" as used in professional sports covers a broad range of relationships with an athlete. An agent may simply be a personal friend—a family lawyer, a teacher, or a coach—who offers advice on a contract negotiation. At the other extreme, an agent may be part of an international conglomerate that handles all financial matters for the athlete. Most agents fill a role somewhere between friend and all-purpose management firm.

For purposes of the NCAA rules that forbid a student-athlete from retaining an agent, any person who intends to market the athlete's skills or reputation is considered an agent. California, the only state that explicitly regulates sports agents, defines an agent as any person who (1) solicits an athlete to enter an agency contract or any professional team sports contract, or (2) for a fee, offers, promises, or attempts to help someone obtain a job with a professional sports team. This does not include employees of professional teams. Agents for athletes in individual sports, such as golf and tennis, apparently are not covered by the California law.

In some respects the sports agent has a parallel in the entertainment industry. An actor may have a personal manager, a booking agent, a lawyer, and an accountant. A lawyer or accountant, in addition to providing professional services, may also serve in a managerial or agent role. The actor's agent seeks outlets for the client's talents. The agent for a star actor, for example, may buy a script suited to his client and then package the script and the actor for a deal with a producer or studio.

Actors generally do not have long-term exclusive commitments to a particular studio. Team sports athletes, however, are usually tied to one team. That team has the sole rights to use the athlete's professional skills for a period of years. This makes the function of a team sports agent much narrower than that of an entertainment agent. The athlete usually has a job, or at least a team, and the conditions of employment have been settled through collective bargaining. The sports agent's primary role is limited to bargaining for money and length of contract and occasionally for special rights such as a no-trade clause.

Like an actor, an athlete can capitalize on his name through product endorsements, public appearances, and other business opportunities. Agents provide expert advice and seek and sift through offers in this area. This function is particularly important for agents of individual sports athletes, such as golfers, tennis players, skiers, and runners.

In addition to contract negotiation and trading on the athlete's name, professional advisors offer athletes financial planning and tax counseling. This area requires the advice of lawyers, accountants, and investment experts. The term "agent" is rarely used to refer to these people unless they also negotiate the athlete's playing contract.

Although some lawyers who represent athletes object to being described as agents, the term "sports agent" is commonly used to refer to anyone who negotiates playing contracts. This book focuses on them.

Question 2: Why agents now?

Before negotiating his 1967 contract, Detroit Tigers pitcher Earl Wilson did something very unusual: He mapped out his goals and strategy with an attorney. Wilson, as was customary, entered general manager Jim Campbell's office alone, but whenever an unanticipated snag arose, he excused himself, walked outside to a telephone booth, and called his apartment. His attorney answered the phone.

"Certainly, I would have preferred to be with Earl in the flesh," recalled his attorney. "But at that time it would have been impossible." Today the collective bargaining agreement of each team sport ensures that management will negotiate with a player's representative.

Wilson was not the first athlete to have an agent. The most famous football player of the 1920s, Red Grange, signed a contract to play with the Chicago Bears the day after his last college game for Illinois in 1925. His agent C.C. (Cash and Carry) Pyle negotiated the deal, which guaranteed the Galloping Ghost at least $100,000 for eight games in eleven days that fall. But it is only during the last decade that agents have captured a pervasive, and occasionally perverse, role in professional sports.

The rise of the agent has coincided with undreamed of increases in players' salaries. It is not the agents, but rather the drastically increased bargaining power of the athletes that makes most of the financial gains possible.

Two factors primarily account for the players' stronger position. First, in the 1970s, competition from new leagues against the established leagues in football, basketball, and hockey pushed up salary packages. Second, the opportunity to enter the open market as a free agent—won by collective bargaining, legal suits, and arbitrators' decisions—gives players the threat of an alternative to accepting the owner's final offer. And multimillion-dollar national television contracts and increasing cable television revenues provide the owners with the ability to offer higher salaries. Agents, ideally, help athletes take advantage of their bargaining power.*

John Claiborne, who negotiated many of the Boston Red Sox contracts immediately before and after the end of the old reserve system under which baseball players were bound to their team until traded or released, reflected on the new management-player relationship at the bargaining table:

---

*For additional information on salaries, including recent salary schedules for some of the major sports, see Appendix B.

No longer do you have the high ground over the player. He has more control over his destiny than the club. Before, you told the player, "Here is what I want to give you." He said, "I don't want it." The owner, sooner or later, would say, "take it or leave and [don't play]." Now the player can say, "I'm leaving."

The agent can help the player decide when to tell the general manager "I'm leaving" or when to say "Add another year at $200,000 and I'll stay." The agent can help his client negotiate not only for more compensation, but for a package of financial terms best suited to his client's needs. Such a package may include a bonus for signing, deferred compensation to be paid ten years later for the next five years, and annual payments to a trust fund for the education of the player's children. For example, Dave Winfield's ten-year contract with the New York Yankees reportedly includes $25,000 bonuses each year he plays 130 games or wins a Gold Glove, and annual payments by the owner to the Dave Winfield Foundation, a charity organization Winfield sponsors. Some players prefer only a signing bonus and annual salaries. Most athletes who are offered contracts by major league teams have some flexibility in negotiating their mix of bonus, deferred compensation, and straight salary.

Occasionally contracts include more exotic items. Gus Williams signed a five-year contract with Seattle for about $700,000 a year plus a $172,000 white Rolls Royce. Pete Rose received offers of a beer distributorship from an owner in the brewing business and an interest in a horse breeding farm when he was a free agent. First baseman Dan Meyer's contract with the Oakland A's guarantees that he won't be given a hotel room above the fifth floor. Guard Otis Birdsong had a contract with the Cleveland Cavaliers (before he was traded to the New York Nets) which would pay him 50 cents for every ticket sold between 5,000 and 15,000 each game plus an $850,000 annual salary. Kareem Abdul-Jabbar's four-year $3,699,500 contract (through 1982-83) includes the use of the L.A. Forum one day each year. Generally, such special provisions are limited to those players with the most bargaining leverage.

In addition, it is increasingly common for contracts to require the team to pay the athlete's tuition for college or graduate school during the off-season or a bonus upon graduation. One agent has dubbed this "the Mama clause" because it makes the player's mother happy. Players and management agree that these incentives for an athlete to complete his education are mutually beneficial. Some agents, however, are less enthusiastic about negotiating for educational incentives because it is difficult for the agent to claim a percentage of the educational payment as part of his fee. Baseball has a college scholarship plan which any player may enter if his club agrees. The NFL, at the urging of the NCAA, has begun to encourage its clubs to offer educational incentives.

Most of these special features were unheard of before the salary escalation that began in the mid-1960s. When a player earned $10,000 or even $20,000 there was not enough money involved for the player to worry about how to package his compensation. His team held lifetime rights to him. He could not become a free agent. For most players it would not have paid to hire an agent who—if the owner or general manager would talk to him—might wangle an additional $500 or even $1,000. Although star athletes earned salaries large enough to justify an agent's services even in the 1960s, most players negotiated their own deals.

Question 3: What can an agent do for me?

A good agent can help a player in several ways. The agent can:
- determine the value of the player's services;
- convince a club to pay the player that value;
- shape the package of compensation to suit the player's needs;

- protect the player's rights under his contract and within the sport's basic agreement and rules;
- counsel the player about postcareer security, both financial and occupational;
- find a new club for a free agent;
- help the athlete earn extra income from endorsements, speeches, and commercials;
- advise an athlete as to how his personal conduct may affect his career.

A good agent generally allows the athlete to concentrate on performing.

A competent agent knows the current market value for players with characteristics similar to those of his client. One football agent explained to a *New York Times* reporter:

> Recently some club told me, "Well there are no defensive linemen who make $100,000 a year." When somebody tells me that, I know five of them whom I represent. And they can't handle that. So it takes away the kinds of arguments they normally use.

Management of professional teams—regardless of what they may tell an agent about other players' salaries—usually have access to contract information about players on other teams (sometimes supplied by agents). One agent illustrated this point at a meeting of the Association of Representatives of Professional Athletes (ARPA). After the agent had negotiated a contract with the Kansas City Chiefs, he flew immediately to St. Louis. Two hours after finishing the Chiefs' contract, he sat with the Cardinals' general manager to discuss another player's contract. The Cardinals knew all the details of the Chiefs' deal.

The professional leagues do not rely only on word-of-mouth for salary information. They are increasingly systematizing the collection of contract data for their teams. The players' associations, particularly in football and baseball, offer detailed contract information to their members (and their agents, if the player so authorizes). Their information, however, is not always current. Since many players, especially in the NFL, are reluctant to talk about their contracts with other players, having an informed agent at the bargaining table can be critical.

In addition to knowing what other comparable players are being paid, a good agent offers two attributes which most players lack: detailed *knowledge* of the right of his client under his contract and his sport's basic agreement (between the teams and the players' union) and the *skills* of an experienced negotiator. For example, when the New York Mets traded pitcher Jon Matlack to the Texas Rangers, his lawyer-agent forced the Mets to comply with a rule in the basic agreement requiring the old team either to pay any future bonuses previously negotiated or to agree with the player on an adjustment. Matlack received more than $100,000 even though he may not have met the performance criteria for earning the bonuses had he stayed with the Mets.

A skilled agent will gauge his client's leverage. For a high-round football or basketball draft choice, some of the factors the agent will assess are:

- Does the team have any other high draft choices?
- Is the local press putting pressure on the team?
- If the team traded for the draft right used to pick the player, who did they give up and what is his salary?
- How important is it to this client's ability to succeed that he sign quickly and avoid missing any part of preseason training?
- How is the team's position on the contract and its attitude toward the player likely to be affected by prolonged negotiation?

Psychologically, an agent may be more effective than an athlete in negotiations. As one agent observed, "It's very difficult to represent yourself unless you're a total egotist." Moreover, since most team owners negotiate through their agents—the general managers—an athlete who negotiates his own deal puts himself at a disadvantage. Once a principal (the player or owner) makes a statement in a negotiation, he becomes bound by that statement. This is not so with agents, who are free in their discussions to explore the boundaries of any negotiation detail. Even if the owner personally negotiates, a young athlete may feel intimidated in talking with an older, experienced businessman.

Negotiating through an agent may avoid the creation of personal hard feelings between a player and the owner or general manager. The agent can take the blame as the "bad guy" and shield the athlete from harsh comments made in the heat of negotiations.

Agents often serve a valuable role as counselor. Agents help their clients adjust to problems—professional and personal. "My agent was a good friend and steadying influence on me," Rudy Tomjanovich said, commenting on his 13-year NBA career. "You need that in a league where the emotions run from red hot to ice cold." Some agents won't hesitate to tell their clients when (and why) the player is wrong in a dispute with the team. An agent may lay out the options for a strategic decision: "What are the risks and rewards of playing out my option?" or "What education and job experience should I pursue in the off-season in order to prepare for a good job after I retire from sports?" One baseball agent advised his clients to volunteer for community service work during the 1981 players' strike. An agent might encourage a client to attend an optional early training camp or to hone his skills in an off-season league.

An agent frequently offers financial guidance (on budgeting, taxes, and investments) for players who lack the time, desire, or capacity to handle their money judiciously. This aspect is discussed in Question 6.

Finally, a good agent knows when he needs help. Even the most experienced, informed agents will not try to handle an unusually complex contract alone. When both Buffalo of the

NBA and an American Basketball League team were bidding for guard Ernie DiGregorio, his agent-lawyer called on a California tax lawyer whose clients include top movie stars, an investment counselor who was head of one of the largest investment banking firms, and a law firm to draft the contract. The agent knew from ten years' experience in representing basketball players that his client needed a skilled and experienced team of advisers to deal with the Buffalo owner's lawyers and advisers.

In summary, a good agent does more than help a player convert his athletic skills into financial security. He protects his client's rights and, as New York Yankee executive Cedric Tallis said, "keeps the player in a frame of mind where he can perform best for himself and his team."

Question 4: How does someone qualify to be an agent?

> There are no standards, no qualifications. The only qualification is that you have a client.
> —A prominent baseball attorney-agent and former counsel to the Major League Baseball Players Association

Some men even try to act as agents without any clients. A Seattle attorney, for example, offered to represent two Seattle Seahawks. Although neither accepted, the attorney called the football team and said he represented the two players. One of the players eventually signed a contract without this lawyer's help. The lawyer still sent the player a bill for $3,000. The player, who denied even talking to the lawyer, did not pay the bill.

Since all it takes to be an agent is a client, agents have backgrounds in a variety of fields. While many agents have studied law, others may have experience as accountants, real estate brokers, used car salesmen, teachers, coaches, bankers, building contractors, public relations directors, dentists, kosher caterers, dry cleaners, or professional athletes. One West Coast lawyer-agent compared the field to the Wild, Wild West. He told a *Washington Post* reporter:

> Anyone can be an agent. Every frustrated jock, every accountant who is bored, every lawyer who is doing pig iron contracts feels that athletic representation could be a lot more exciting, and it offers some vicarious thrills. The Hillside Strangler could be an agent.

The lack of requirements for those entering the business as sports agents forces each athlete to make his own evaluation of a prospective agent's qualifications. One important but not essential qualification is knowledge of the law. Since many agents have attended law school, it is important to consider some of the less obvious implications of an agent's having a legal background.

As the Seattle incident confirms, a law degree does not ensure honesty. Neither is it a guarantee that a lawyer is familiar with the law relevant to sports representation. In reviewing the seminars for agents sponsored by the NFL Players Association, a junior staff member commented, "basically good lawyers would be asking questions that seemed elementary to me."

A former counsel to the NBA Players Association found a similar problem among basketball agents:

> A lot of people hold themselves out as being knowledgeable and competent. But the questions we get from individuals who purport to represent players are shocking. They don't understand player contracts, the collective bargaining agreement, or they simply don't understand the industry.

Some lawyer-agents do not keep up with changes in the law. An attorney for an NFL team recalled negotiating a contract with a lawyer-agent who did not understand the tax laws dealing with maximum tax on earned income, an important provision for athletes. As a result, the attorney said, "he was insisting on a deferred income plan which would have been good a few years earlier."

Most agents with legal training are both honest and competent, but many are not practicing lawyers. Some agents with legal degrees did not take or pass a state bar exam and therefore are not licensed to practice law. Others gave up legal practice. These agents generally do not feel bound by the code of ethics that applies to practicing lawyers. This does not mean that such agents are unethical; rather, it frees them to compete more aggressively for clients with non-lawyer agents. Practicing lawyers are not allowed to solicit clients by direct personal contact or by paying another person to contact a prospective client.

The tradeoff for an attorney who holds himself out as an agent rather than as a practicing attorney is that state law prohibits him from giving legal advice. While the agent clearly cannot represent an athlete in court, other limits on his activities are harder to define and vary from state to state. In some states, for example, he cannot draft a contract for the sale of the player's house.

A player who has any doubts about an agent's status as a lawyer should not hesitate to ask him. A legal diploma or a bar admittance certificate hanging on an agent's wall does not necessarily mean that he is a practicing attorney. If any doubt lingers about his status, contact the local bar association.

The following profiles illustrate the variety of ways in which agents combine law and athlete representation. (The names are changed.)

Arthur has added athlete clients to his existing corporate law practice in Beverly Hills. He is in his mid-thirties, fit, plays a lot of tennis (as the trophies in his office attest). He says he represents a few Los Angeles Dodgers as "an interest of the heart. I do it because I enjoy it and I think I can be of some help to the people I represent."

Stephen shares Arthur's enthusiasm for working with athletes. But athlete clients, mostly hockey and a few baseball players, provide most of his legal practice. Stephen claims to be the world's foremost expert on American college hockey over the last 15 years. He practices law with one partner in a simple office near Fifth Avenue in midtown Manhattan.

Sam, in contrast, runs his athlete management firm from a plush office suite in Boston. Although he likes to refer to himself as a sports lawyer and retains informal ties to a law firm, Sam devotes full time to his management firm in an agent capacity. He represents athletes in all four major sports, a rather unusual situation. Sam has participated in more than 1,800 contract negotiations for more than 300 clients in 15 years.

Jack, an associate with a corporate law firm in a midwestern city, was a good enough amateur golfer to have qualified for and played in the United States Open. He began to represent professional golfers and now his sports management company has three offices in the United States and offices in England, Belgium, Monte Carlo, Japan, Hong Kong, Australia, New Zealand, and Brazil.

Dan has two separate jobs. He practices law part time with a firm in New York (which has no sports ties), and he represents athletes through a management corporation based in a suburb of New York. After serving as general counsel to a baseball team for about 18 months after graduating from law school, he and the team's relations director resigned to set up their own management firm. Most of their business in the first year came from handling commercial endorsements rather than from negotiating playing contracts.

Joe got into athlete representation after law school because he helped the basketball coach at his college recruit high school players in Chicago. The coach provided him with his first client. Now he handles contract negotiations, taxes, investments, and occasionally house closings and vacations for basketball players and a few football players. Some of his clients call him Uncle Joe.

Harry is a lawyer and a certified public accountant. His office is in a Southern college town where he has close ties to the football program. He represents only football players and his services include direct handling of all their money. "It takes the pressure off of them, especially from demands of family, who think their rich cousin should share with all his relatives."

In summary, many agents have degrees in law or accounting. But since there are absolutely no requirements for entering the field, an athlete should scrutinize carefully the qualifications of any prospective agent. Part II of this book elaborates on how to find and select an agent.

Question 5: Should I represent myself?

After hitting .318 in 1980, Cleveland Indians catcher Ron Hassey negotiated his own contract and signed for $165,000. That same year New York Yankee catcher Rick Cerone, represented by an agent, won a $450,000 salary through arbitration.

Detroit Tiger shortstop Alan Trammell decided to represent himself and negotiated a seven-year $2.8 million contract before the 1981 season. Trammell, 22, reportedly wanted to save the agent's fee and had been upset by going through arbitration the previous year. Trammell's teammate, Steve Kemp, retained an agent and won a one-year $600,000 contract for 1981 in arbitration after the team rejected his proposal for a long-term agreement. The attorney-agent used a series of charts to show that Kemp was one of baseball's most productive hitters.

Hassey and Trammell are exceptions. Nearly all major league

athletes retain agents. Most high-round basketball and football draft choices, some hockey and baseball amateur draft picks, and most major league athletes can benefit from professional advice before signing a playing contract. A telephone conversation with an agent before facing the general manager directly may be sufficient in some situations, but generally full representation is required.

Sometimes an athlete and his agent plot their negotiating strategy to appear as if the athlete is acting on his own. Scott Perry, an NFL defensive back, has used this ploy because, he and his agent calculated, "they give you more if you play nice, suck in your pride, and don't bring an agent." One experienced and shrewd baseball executive, after suggesting that if a player is sharp enough he should represent himself, conceded that he prefers to negotiate directly with a player because the team will do better than if an agent had represented the athlete.

A player should represent himself in certain circumstances. An athlete with little bargaining power and a small salary often neither needs nor can afford an agent. For example, since most minor league baseball players play under standard rate contracts, an agent would have trouble justifying any fee. He might offer to represent a player throughout his minor league career for no charge *except* for the right to represent him if the player advances to the major leagues. A player who signed such an agreement would be binding himself without gaining any real benefit. A minor league or college athlete should be especially wary of any agent who offers gifts or loans as an inducement to sign an agreement with him.

Occasionally a player will recognize that he may be better off if he settles for a salary less than what an agent might be able to obtain. In this case, he may not need an agent. For example, a fringe player may be able to prolong his career by not trying to squeeze out the top dollars. Louis Dampier credited his survival in the NBA to keeping his price tag down while other players, some more skilled, priced themselves out of the NBA. A player who recognizes that he is in a similar situation may be better off negotiating his own contract and saving the agent's fee.

An agent for a fringe player can play a role similar to an agent for a bit actor. Consider Mickey Lolich, who sat out a season rather than complete the second year of a two-year contract with the New York Mets. In the course of working out a contract problem between the San Diego Padres and pitcher Bob Owchinko, Lolich's (and Owchinko's) attorney-agent mentioned that Lolich might want to pitch again. The 37-year-old Lolich eventually signed with the Padres. Agents for basketball players who play in Europe or for American football players who go to the Canadian Football League are other examples of the placement role agents play for fringe players.

For most major league athletes and college basketball and football players after their eligibility expires (and for some before), professional advice usually pays—providing it comes from a competent and honest person. Management, which formerly tried hard to induce the player to deal directly with the owner or general manager, now generally accepts agents as playing a legitimate role. But the player's choice of agent may influence—for better or worse—management's attitude toward the player. After the 1981 season, for example, the Tigers traded Steve Kemp to the White Sox for Chet Lemon rather than face another possible arbitration, reportedly because Detroit preferred negotiating with Lemon's agent rather than with Kemp's agent. Which agent represents a player has become a factor that several NFL teams consider in making their first-round draft selection.

Finally, college athletes have one additional constraint. Retaining an agent can cost them their collegiate eligibility. As Iona basketball player Jeff Ruland learned the hard way, National Collegiate Athletic Association rules forbid an eligible athlete to sign *any* agreement with an agent, or to agree orally to be represented by an agent, or to accept cash or gifts from an agent.

Question 6: What other professional advice do I need?

If the agent succeeds in helping a player earn more money from his athletic skills, then the athlete may need professional help in managing his finances. The extent of such advice and whether it should come from several independent advisers (tax lawyer, accountant, investment counselor) or from a full-service management firm involve very important and difficult decisions.

An athlete should consider his spending and savings habits, his interest in personal involvement in money management, how much time he can devote to it, his educational background, and his financial experience. Changes in the amount of his income and in his family situation are also important factors. For example, consider the situation of a basketball player who has been sheltered and pampered by coaches and others since junior high school because of his athletic skills. A full-service arrangement in which the athlete signs over his paycheck, has his bills paid and his money invested, and receives an allowance may be well-suited for such an athlete. A team attorney explained:

> Many athletes haven't gone through the basic economic training most of us have received. For example, a basketball player got a notice from the bank saying he was five months behind on his mortgage, and the bank was preparing to foreclose. He took the attitude, "I'm busy playing basketball; I'm good for it. After the season's over, I'll pay." I had to explain to him that the bank's computer doesn't work that way.

Most athletes, especially players who have had to struggle financially for several years on low minor league salaries, are not as financially naive. But almost anybody, athlete or nonathlete, earning even half of the *average* major league salary (more than $100,000) requires accounting assistance, legal services such as tax and estate planning, and financial counseling.

Some investment firms and banks cater their services to athletes. The NBA Players Association, for example, signed an agreement with a major investment firm to provide investment and financial planning services to its members. Such firms may approach an athlete directly or through his agent or attorney.

Some athletes direct the team to send their entire paycheck to their agent or financial manager. The check is still made out to the player, but the agent or financial manager deposits it in a bank account in the athlete's name. The agent pays the athlete an "allowance," pays his bills (including the agent's fee), and invests the remainder (in some cases without the athlete's specific approval).

One respected athlete management firm follows this procedure:

- All checks are deposited into the athlete's account and bills are paid from the account.
- All checks drawn from the account are co-signed and are physically signed by officers of the company.
- Investments normally are made only after the client signs his or her own investment papers.
- On a monthly basis, the client is sent an accounting of everything received in the account and everything paid from the account during the preceding month.
- This accounting is reconciled to the bank statement, and the bank statement and reconciliation are also given to the client on a monthly basis.

One of the advantages of this system is that the company ends up with excellent records for preparing the client's tax returns and for defending the client in the event of a tax audit by the government. In addition, the company can give the client projections of income and outgo over the next year. The difference between income and expenses equals discretionary funds, which can be used for investment. Furthermore, the company can project what the client's income tax will be under different circumstances so that the client is in a position to decide whether or not he wants to make tax-shelter investments.

Before agreeing to any type of financial management arrangement, an athlete should thoroughly investigate—with professional help—the reputation, experience, and results of the agent and his associates as financial managers. An important factor is what bonding or insurance protection the athlete would have if the agent squanders his money.

The terms of the arrangement should be described in a written contract, which is separate from the agreement to negotiate playing contracts.* This agreement should be reviewed by another lawyer. It should specify the agent's services, such as

- general bookkeeping;
- analysis of the player's budget, including an annual financial summary;
- analysis of the player's tax liability and tax planning;
- preparation of tax returns;
- payment of the player's expenses;
- periodic reports of the current status of the player's financial affairs.
- counseling about obtaining related services, such as legal, accounting, estate planning, and insurance.

The agreement should also specify the method and amount of compensation for the agent's time and expenses.

Finally, an athlete considering authorizing his agent to manage his finances should recognize that there are banks, investment firms, and financial planning companies that can provide similar services. Since so many alternatives exist and the potential for abuse is so great, an athlete should not rush into any financial management deal. The athlete should recognize that

---

*Sample contracts between athlete and agent and between athlete and financial manager or investment manager are provided in Appendix C.

his agent—no matter how skilled at negotiating playing contracts—may not be as well qualified to manage his funds. An athlete should ask his agent, accountant, and lawyer each to evaluate and compare several services on his behalf. In addition, the athlete should feel comfortable personally with his investment advisor. This makes it crucial for the athlete to meet with any advisor *before* he retains his firm.

II
Matchmaking—Athlete Meets Agent

Question 7: How do I find an agent?
Question 8: How do I choose an agent?
Question 9: What if I'm thinking about turning pro early?
Question 10: How does signing a power of attorney affect the athlete-agent relationship?
Question 11: Do I need a written agreement?

Question 7: How do I find an agent?

> I needed an attorney, but I didn't know any. I didn't have that problem for long.
>
> —Rudy Tomjanovich, recalling his senior year as a Michigan All-American

The problem is not finding an agent, but finding the right one at the right time. Plenty of agents—although not always the best ones—find the athlete. Some three hundred agents tried to represent Heisman Trophy winner George Rogers. More than a hundred would-be agents contacted quarterback Neil Lomax before the NFL draft. Kansas City Royals relief pitcher Bob Tufts, then an unknown minor leaguer, suddenly received a slew of mail from agents in the midst of an outstanding Class AA season. To get his attention they clipped a copy of his statistics to information about themselves. At least one baseball agent sends emissaries to search the minor leagues for Latin American players and to sign them to complex contracts written in English, not in their native Spanish.

Agents routinely solicit college athletes before or early in their senior year. (The NCAA rule which forbids an athlete to agree to retain an agent until after his senior playing season ends does not restrain the agents.) One agent told a meeting of the Association of Representatives of Professional Athletes (ARPA) that by mid-October he had mailed 269 letters to college football players. He may have been too late. At least one prominent agent has admitted publicly to having signed college athletes before their seasons had ended and to lending them money. He alleged that at least 60 percent of the football players drafted in the top three rounds had made a commitment to an agent before their eligibility expired. In May of 1982, an NFL general manager estimated that three-quarters of the likely 150 top draft choices in the *1983* NFL draft already had agreed to retain an agent. Competition among agents is so fierce that lawyers attending an American Bar Association sports law conference were told that no "ethical" attorney in the audience would be able to represent a first-round NFL draft choice (except possibly if he had a personal connection to the athlete).

One tactic at least one well-known agent has employed is to ask the student-athlete to sign an "offer sheet." The agent promises not to sign the sheet until the athlete has completed his final season; therefore, he maintains, the athlete has not signed a binding contract during the season. Whether or not the athlete has entered a legally binding agreement, the NCAA rules are clear: This is a violation. Any agreement to retain an agent, whether or not written, whether or not legally enforceable, is against NCAA rules.

Some athletes, after signing an offer sheet or a similar piece of paper with one agent, have tried to renege and hire another agent. The result has often been messy and expensive lawsuits. If the athlete still has eligibility remaining, the first agent may threaten to expose his agreement to the university and the NCAA. Richard Sorkin, after his conviction, told a New York State Senate committee that he and other agents signed many athletes to representational agreements before their seasons had ended. He said that in one case he wired the athlete $150 with which to buy a coat, an additional violation of NCAA rules. An athlete who signs with an agent before his college eligibility expires runs the risk of bringing sanctions against himself, his college, or both. Villanova University forfeited its second-place trophy and television revenue from the 1971 NCAA basketball tournament after it was learned that its star, Howard Porter, had signed with an agent prior to the tournament.

Cash or other inducements to sign an agency agreement indicates that an agent lacks the integrity most athletes expect from their agents. An agent allegedly offered running back

George Rogers $5,000 for living expenses during his senior year. One "agent" offered quarterback Neil Lomax "a community residential security plan and private escorts." Some agents hire front men to contact college athletes, often during the summer. These "bird dogs" offer an "inducement" to make the athlete's senior year much more comfortable. The *Boston Globe* reported that in 1982 the inducement for football players was a $15,000 "signing bonus," a car, and a $7,500 wrist watch. After the player signs a professional contract, the agent takes out the $15,000 bonus, funds for the car, his fee (often 10 percent), and his expenses. Another recruiting tactic used by one prominent agent, according to an NFL general manager, was to take college athletes to cocaine parties.

Robert C. James, commissioner of the Atlantic Coast Conference, explained:

> Unscrupulous agents operate by attempting to develop a sense of obligation on the part of the athletes they are trying to recruit. Their approach varies but it may take the form of free tickets to professional games or to other entertainment, lavish dinners, brief vacations, or free travel.

Such tactics should raise a warning flag that this agent may put his own interests ahead of the client's best interests.

The situation differs in individual sports where athletes pay their own expenses and are not guaranteed a salary. Some athletes could not afford to join the professional golf or tennis tour without financial help. For example, in 1973 a sports management company offered to sponsor the United States Amateur Golf Championship winner on the women's professional tour. In return she agreed to repay any advances made for her expenses and to retain the firm as her agent for several years. Many years after her commitment to the firm expired, the same firm still represented Laura Baugh. The firm made a similar arrangement with Tulsa University golfer Nancy Lopez.

Even a recommendation from a coach or a teammate is no guarantee that a particular agent will best represent a particular player. The person who makes the recommendation may have his own special interest at stake. Consider the lawyer-agent in a major city who offered to represent a player *without* charge if, in return, the player solicited other clients. In addition, the agent promised the player a 40 percent share of any fees he collected from the new clients. This arrangement is a flagrant violation of state bar rules against solicitation and fee splitting by lawyers with non-lawyers. After the player brought in five or six clients *and* the agent collected more than $100,000 in fees, the agent denied that any agreement existed and refused to share his fees.

Most agents are smooth talkers. One tactic some agents use is to familiarize themselves with the vernacular of an athlete's home neighborhood. When they meet the athlete they try to impress him with their knowledge about the in-spots, streets, and modes of transportation. George Taliaferro, a former NFL player and, as special assistant to the president of Indiana University, an informal counselor to such athletes as Isiah Thomas, warns college athletes not to be taken in by such glibness.

A letter or phone call from an agent to a college athlete is a legitimate technique for a non-lawyer agent. However, since in most states the bar code of ethics does not allow a lawyer personally to solicit clients, an athlete who wants a practicing lawyer to represent him may have to look a little harder. As one attorney-agent explained, "I can't go down to the dugout and pass out my cards." This puts practicing lawyers at a disadvantage in obtaining athlete clients, since other agents are free to use almost any approach to a prospective client. The attorney elaborated:

> Generally athletes are unsophisticated from a business standpoint. He who gets there first and he who says I have the biggest stable has the greatest chance to sign another one.

However, the relative disadvantage that a practicing lawyer faces in obtaining athlete clients should diminish as a result of a

Supreme Court decision in 1982 which was expected to eliminate many of the restraints on advertising by lawyers.

Lawyers also have indirect means of expressing interest in a prospective client. For example, one New York attorney-agent obtains his basketball clients by recommendations from coaches and other players. His first client, Jim McMillan, came to him on the recommendation of McMillan's coach at Columbia, who had been telephoned by the Yale coach. "I certainly managed to tell the Yale coach I'd be real interested in representing McMillan," the attorney said.

One approach taken by some student-athletes, such as Indiana State star Larry Bird before he signed a $3.15 million, five-year Boston Celtics contract, is to set up a screening committee in the community where the university is situated. The athlete and his family can refer inquiries from agents to the committee. The committee can also invite agents, including attorneys who feel constrained from soliciting, to submit proposals for representing the athlete and can later interview those it finds best qualified and suited for the individual athlete. But the value of screening committees depends heavily on the members' qualifications and commitment to the athlete's best interests.

Question 8: How do I choose an agent?

> Just about every day there's another guy who tells me he's the guy to be my agent. That's the usual line, that he'll do what's best for me.
>
> —Freeman Williams, 1977 and 1978
> college basketball scoring leader
> *The Sporting News*, April 1, 1978

> They all would tell you how good they were . . . how they could beat the system. And they'd bad mouth other agents.
>
> —Kelly Tripucka, Notre Dame forward
> *The Sporting News*, February 13, 1982

How should an outstanding young athlete pick an agent or possibly a team of agents to negotiate his first contract? Some suggestions:

- *Get help.* The combination of the athlete's lack of business experience and the knack of many agents to sweet-talk a prospective client often makes it wise for the athlete to ask his parents, a coach, or a professor to help screen the agents. A hometown lawyer may be valuable in interviewing the athlete's top choices and in reviewing any contract between the athlete and an agent *before* the athlete signs anything. This adviser can also help the athlete determine what services he will require and whether they should be provided by one agent or firm or by a combination of agent, lawyer, accountant, or other specialists. Some athletes are represented by two independent lawyers—a personal lawyer and a sports specialist. Pitcher Fernando Valenzuela retained a baseball specialist to help negotiate his contract with the Dodgers and a Spanish-speaking agent to handle personal endorsements and other matters. Montreal catcher Gary Carter hired a Canadian agent and an American agent and two tax attorneys from each country to help put together a reported $15 million, eight-year deal.
- Don't rely solely on educational background or titles such as lawyer, financial consultant, or certified public accountant. As one agent quipped, "incompetence spans the educational and occupational horizons."
- Ask a prospective agent for *proof* of his educational background, training, work experience—particularly in the sports field. If the agent is to manage your money, his experience and record for other clients is crucial.
- Ask for character and professional *references* from his clients and persons such as a lawyer not involved in sports, an accountant, or a law school professor if the agent is a young attorney. Talk with those references. Find out how long the clients have been with him.

Matchmaking—Athlete Meets Agent

- Be wary of an agent who advises a football player to change positions to help his chances of getting drafted or tells a basketball player he should shoot more and pass less. Most reputable agents won't try to interfere with a college program in this manner.
- Inquire about a particular agent's *reputation*, through the players' association, other players, and even other agents. Try to speak with former clients to find out why they are former and not current clients. Otherwise, you may find yourself in the situation of the college senior who met a guy who claimed to be a law student and promised he could do a good job negotiating an NBA contract. The athlete called him one night and his wife said he was working at the Y. Assuming that the "law student" was working out at squash or in the weight room after a long day of studying, he called the Y. He discovered that the would-be agent was "doing LAW"—as in cleaning Lavatories And Windows.
- If the agent will handle any of the athlete's funds, find out if he is *bonded*. While bonding is not essential and may not indicate anything about the agent's ability, it is an important factor to consider in evaluating the safety of trusting an agent with substantial amounts of money.
- *Question the agent* in detail about his fees, his relationships with club management, the likely impact of his other clients on your interests, his policy on renegotiating a contract, the length of his contract with you, circumstances under which you can dismiss him, whether he feels bound by any code of ethics, and any other topic that seems at all relevant.
- *Reject* an agent who seems more concerned with quick cash than with your long-term best interests. Some signs of this type of agent are:
  —his clients usually sign contracts very soon after being drafted (because he fears the client will leave him for another agent);
  —he talks more about bonus money (because he can take his cut out of the bonus) than other terms of the agree-

ment, such as salary guarantees or length of contract (shorter may be better because the player can prove himself and then negotiate a better contract);
— he is more interested in collecting his 10 to 20 percent of an excessive fee he has insisted on for a speaking engagement for his athlete-client than in considering whether the athlete will benefit more from the exposure to the audience and the goodwill he might generate.

- If the agent is not a practicing attorney, make sure he agrees to having a lawyer of your choice review your playing contract or any investment agreements. Even if such a review is not necessary, a reputable agent will not object to your retaining the option to consult an attorney before signing any legal documents.

- Avoid an agent who offers money or gifts as an inducement to sign, especially if his contract is for several years. Any money an athlete receives before signing, he will unknowingly pay back many times over. However tempting the money may look at the time, in most cases the agent will manipulate your money later to recoup anything he gave you for signing.

- Be wary of outrageous claims by agents such as:
  — "I represent many star athletes." Check this out carefully.
  — "I can get you $1 million." Ask him how much will be cash and how much will be guaranteed.
  — "I can get you drafted in the first round."
  — "You will not get drafted without my help."
  — "I will make you millions in investments in three or four years."
  — "I guarantee to make you rich."
  — "You will not ever have to pay taxes."
  — "I will put you into oil wells, and I've never had a dry hole."
  — Anything that sounds too fantastic to be true.

- Ask any agent who promises merchandising deals what

deals he has gotten and for whom. There are few opportunities for team sports athletes.
- Avoid an agent who by his own practice or admission is violating certain rules or laws. If he is willing to cheat others openly, what will stop him from cheating you?
- Look for an agent who will take the time to explain his answer to any question you ask. One good test of his understanding of the business aspects of the sport and his ability to articulate his knowledge is to ask him for a thorough explanation of the players' pension plan.

Individual sports athletes should ask several additional questions, all designed to find out what the agent knows about the sport, worldwide, and the people who are involved in the sport at all levels.

- Can my agent represent me in connection with business affairs that are, literally, worldwide in scope? Does my agent have experience in negotiating equipment contracts? Apparel contracts? Does he know the advertising agencies? The equipment manufacturers? What is his track record in these areas? What are the logistics?

Choosing an agent is one of the most important decisions an athlete makes. It is a process that an athlete cannot afford to take lightly. The athlete has a wide choice of agents—some competent, some incompetent—competing for few available clients and the prospect of glamour, glory, and riches. The athlete should not rush into a decision; he should decide only after consulting parents, coaches, other players, and a nonagent lawyer. Finally, the athlete must feel comfortable with the person representing him.

Question 9: What if I'm thinking about turning pro early?

Questions about retaining an agent pose special problems for student-athletes who consider turning professional before their class graduates. Ralph Sampson reportedly rejected $3.8 million over six years from the NBA after his sophomore year at Virginia, and he turned down the prospect of an even better contract after his junior year. Isiah Thomas, Mark Aguirre, Magic Johnson, and James Worthy chose to leave school early for pro basketball. Herschel Walker seriously considered signing with the Canadian Football League after nearly winning the Heisman Trophy as a freshman. He considered trying to play in the NFL after his sophomore year, but decided to stay at Georgia at least one more year. While most of the attention has focused on undergraduate basketball players deciding whether to turn pro early, if Walker or another outstanding underclassman decides to sign a professional football contract before his class graduates, a situation similar to that in basketball could quickly develop for college football players. The United States Football League stated that it would not sign underclassmen for its initial season in 1983. But either competition between the NFL and the USFL or a suit by an underclassman could change the situation.

If professional football teams start signing undergraduates, college players will need to be wary of agents who push them to sign early without thoroughly evaluating the pros and cons of that decision. Basketball players have faced the same decision since Spencer Haywood went to court in 1971 to force the NBA to sign undergraduates.

Consider the case of Yommi Sangodeyi, a 6 foot 10 inch, 240 pound *reserve* center for Sam Houston State. After Sangodeyi's sophomore year, an adviser convinced him to sign a letter to the NBA asking to be drafted in the June 1982 draft. His only realistic hope of making the NBA was to stay in college. Before the draft Sangodeyi asked the NCAA to restore his eligibility because he thought he had signed only to go to tryout sessions and summer camps. After two hearings, the NCAA restored his eligibility on the basis that Sangodeyi had misunderstood the letter and had no intent to become a pro. The NCAA also determined that the adviser was not an agent, but had acted only as a friend who had known Sangodeyi since the adviser was a Peace Corps volunteer in Nigeria. An NCAA attorney described the case as probably the only circumstances in which an undergraduate who asked to be placed on the draft list could regain his eligibility.

The interplay of the NCAA rules, designed to protect the amateur concept, and the NBA draft procedure make the talented basketball player's situation extremely sensitive and difficult. Under NBA rules enacted after the 1981 season, teams may not contact an undergraduate unless he has placed his name on the NBA draft list. But once he has done so, he forfeits his collegiate eligibility.

Consider the situation in which a Ralph Sampson or a Pat Ewing finds himself after his sophomore or junior year. He may choose to stay in school another year, or to place his name on the NBA draft list. At stake for him may be hundreds of thousands or even millions of dollars, his college degree, and his overall well-being. At stake for the agent who becomes his representative may be 5 to 10 percent of that amount. At stake for his college coach may be the opportunity for his team to play in the final four of the NCAA tournament, or a losing season and maybe his job. At stake for the university are the hundreds of thousands of dollars that an All-American basketball player can help generate through gate receipts, television revenue, and tournament revenues. At stake for the NBA teams that would like to draft the player may be the ability to win a division title or even keep the franchise solvent. In sum, the student-athlete's decision may have a cumulative *multi-million-dollar* impact.

Where can the student-athlete with only a year or two of college education turn for help in reaching his decision? What help can he receive without violating NCAA rules? He can talk to agents, but he cannot agree to retain one. As one college coach noted, many agents (especially those with few clients) will encourage the athlete to leave school because that is the only way the agent gets paid. The athlete can hire a lawyer, but only if the lawyer charges his normal fees. The lawyer can review offers (if there are any), he can return the contract, but he cannot make any counteroffers. The athlete can ask his coach to help, but the coach probably is not experienced in making major business deals, may be leery of violating NCAA rules, and has a vested interest in the athlete's staying in school.

One of the most respected college basketball coaches, Dean Smith of the University of North Carolina, told *Washington Post* reporter John Feinstein:

> I think any young man making a decision like that should have the advice of counsel. I don't think it has to be an agent. It can be a family attorney or longtime friend who genuinely has his best interests in mind. The players who left school early and had problems are, for the most part, the ones who left without really knowing what they could get.

An undergraduate football player, such as a Herschel Walker, will need more legal advice than simply being told what kind of contract he can expect. He will need an experienced antitrust lawyer to advise him on the process of challenging the NFL rule against signing undergraduates and on the likelihood of succeeding. He may even need a labor lawyer for advice on how negotiations between the players' union and management will affect the terms of any contract. The situation will become even more complex and the stakes higher if the new United States Football League signs undergraduates who would otherwise be eligible to play college football.

The athlete should also talk with former teammates about their experiences as professionals. Their advice as to whether the athlete may benefit more by playing another year in college or whether he is ready to cope with the life of a professional athlete might be vital.

One of the risks of staying in college is that an injury will diminish or even eliminate an athlete's professional value. One way to limit the potentially devastating impact of an injury is to purchase insurance. Before purchasing such insurance, an athlete should be sure that he has not obtained the money for the premium in any way that violates the NCAA rules.

In summary, the student-athlete who is considering turning pro before his college class graduates should try to become as informed as possible and should be counseled by an attorney.

Question 10: How does signing a power of attorney affect the athlete-agent relationship?

A power of attorney is a written document by which one person (the athlete) appoints another person (who may not necessarily be an attorney) as his legal representative or agent and gives that agent authority to perform certain acts or kinds of acts on the athlete's behalf, such as signing contracts and incurring debts. The document serves as evidence to other parties that the agent has the athlete's authority to act.

An athlete should never sign a power of attorney that is not explicitly limited *in writing* to specific acts or kinds of acts and that is not limited in time or not otherwise subject to termination by the athlete. Before signing any power of attorney, the athlete should be sure he completely understands what he is doing. In most cases, he should consult an uninvolved lawyer before signing.

No matter what an agent says, a power of attorney to handle all investments is *not* standard procedure. Basketball players World Free and Johnny Neumann found that out the hard way. Both signed powers of attorney. Besides negotiating two contracts for Free with the 76ers, his agent incorporated Free into "All-World Enterprises" and bought a sporting goods store and residential property and leased numerous cars. Less than three years later, creditors rang Free's phone constantly and banks lined up for a crack at Free's paycheck. The cars went back, the store closed, and the creditors went to court. Two years after Neumann signed an estimated $1.9 million playing contract and gave two agents power of attorney to invest his money, he filed for bankruptcy and the agents had disappeared.

Legally, with or without any powers of attorney, the agent is the athlete's fiduciary: He must act only in the athlete's best interest. The precise requirements imposed on a fiduciary, who need not be a lawyer, are controlled by state law. One attorney-agent explained that under California law, for example, an agent as fiduciary:

> is bound by a number of rules which restrict him from such things as obtaining secret profits, taking a position adverse to the interest of his principal [the athlete, and] making less than a full disclosure of all material facts in any transaction affecting his client relationship, and which require him to treat his client with the utmost good faith and diligence as is required of a trustee.

Unfortunately, an athlete cannot assume that his agent will always fulfill his fiduciary obligations. Consider the plight of two 21-year-old hockey players who each signed long-term agreements with a management firm. About a year later an accountant for the athletes decided to consult a Chicago law firm about possible mistreatment by the management firm. "If anyone had done any work for them, he should have been sued for malpractice," said the attorney who reviewed both athletes' situations. After reading the attorney's memorandum, the accountant advised the athletes to break their contracts. The management firm responded by threatening to enforce their agreements in court. The players retained new representatives and their attorneys eventually settled the dispute with the management firm.

Obviously when the relationship between agent and athlete becomes so strained that the agent goes to court to enforce the representational agreement, the essence of the agent-client relationship is gone. The athlete must feel confident in placing his full trust in the agent. "Trust is probably the single most important element in an athlete's relationship [with his agent],"

Keith Magnuson, later coach and then captain of the Chicago Black Hawks, told a reporter. "I want to be able to devote all my energies to the game. . . . Knowing that my future and the future of my family is secure enables me to do this." Magnuson explained that his attorney-agent earned his trust by frequently explaining what he was doing for Magnuson and involving him in the decision making. Another agent took a different approach. He carried a business card which read: "In Abdul We Trust."

Even if 90 percent of the agents are honest and competent—as one NFL general manager has estimated—the athlete must be extremely leery of entering a relationship with an unfamiliar agent. The other 10 percent is a constantly changing cast of characters, many of whom have vanished after having taken advantage of trusting young athletes. Until an agent has proven his competency and honesty, an athlete should exercise extreme care in granting him the power of attorney, and even then any power of attorney should be only for purposes specified in writing.

Question 11: Do I need a written agreement?

Several major league baseball players were surprised to discover they had been traded—not to another team, but to another agent. The contract they signed with their agent, which they did not understand, allowed the agent to assign his clients to other agents.

It is crucial for the athlete and agent to reach a precise and clear understanding of the services the agent will provide, and on what basis, before the athlete authorizes the agent to act on his behalf. Among the points which should be discussed are the following:

- What services is the agent to perform? (negotiate contracts for playing services? investment management? personal finance management?)

- Will there be separate contracts for each type of service?
- What is the cost of each of the agent's services?
- Is the agent the only one who can negotiate the playing contract? If he doesn't, does he still get paid? (This is called an exclusive contract.)
- Will the agent have an exclusive right to handle other contracts, such as speeches and product endorsements?
- How long is the agent working for you?
- Are there any renewal provisions?
- What if you want to terminate the agreement?
- If you sign with the agent, is there a "cooling off" period (five to ten days) during which you can withdraw without obligation?
- Who is responsible for the agent's expenses?
- How and when does the agent get paid?
- What about bonuses, playoff money, and awards?
- How are disputes between you and your agent to be settled?
- Are you signing a power of attorney?
- Is this agreement the entire agreement between you and your agent?
- How is this agreement to be evidenced: written contract, retainer letter from the agent, memorandum, a handshake?

First, the player and the agent should agree orally about the nature and extent of their relationship. Then consider a written contract. A written agreement helps ensure that both parties understand their responsibilities and commitments. It may protect the player if he later believes the agent is not fulfilling his duty.

Although an athlete who has been wronged by his agent normally would have a better chance of proving his case in court if he has a written contract, a written agreement is no guarantee of satisfactory service or accountability. It could be useless against a fly-by-night agent or an agent who goes bankrupt. Moreover, a contract could contain provisions detrimental to the player. For example, if it covers too many years, it could prevent him from changing agents despite a legitimate reason to do so.

A written agreement may contain an exclusivity clause under which a former agent will claim a percentage of all the player's endorsement contracts, including ones in which he had no part in arranging. Regardless of whether the agreement includes an exclusivity clause, an athlete who changes agents should recognize that normally he will be liable to pay his former agent at least for the reasonable value of that agent's services up to that point.

He may owe more. After Darryl Dawkins signed a reported $700,000 multi-year contract with the Philadelphia '76ers, his former agent sued Dawkins and his new agent for $1 million plus a percentage of all compensation Dawkins receives under the contract. The former agent claimed that Dawkins breached his contract with him by allowing another agent to negotiate for him. The suit was still pending in 1982.

Some respected agents, including many lawyer-agents, reject the idea of a contract between player and agent. One such agent, for example, has never had a written agreement with any of his three hundred clients. Another considers a long-term agency contract abhorrent to the nature of representing someone. He likened it to a doctor refusing to treat a patient unless the patient agreed not to see any other doctor for three years. A contract between an attorney and an athlete for legal services might violate legal ethics rules. However, even a lawyer's fee structure and basic commitment should be stated in a letter. While this does not bind the athlete to the lawyer, it sets forth the basis for determining the lawyer's compensation and obligation and can lessen the chances of misunderstandings. An agreement to manage an athlete's finances should always be in writing.

In summary, two points are essential in choosing an agent: First, don't rush. An athlete should not agree to any representational arrangement until he has a precise understanding of his relationship with the particular agent. Second, usually there will be a written agreement, either a formal contract or a letter setting forth the basis for the relationship. The athlete should ask an uninvolved attorney to review this agreement and to explain its meaning to him in detail before he signs it.

III
Paying the Agent

Question 12: How much will it cost me?
Question 13: When do I pay?
Question 14: Should the agent collect his fee directly from the club?

Question 12: How much will it cost me?

> There are hundreds of people constantly running after players. They sign them to outrageous kinds of agency contracts—7 ½ to 10 percent of all earnings for extraordinary lengths of time. People are pigs, taking advantage of fairly innocent players.
>
> —A baseball attorney-agent

Not all agents are pigs, but all do charge for their services. The four most commonly used methods of calculating fees for negotiating a contract are as follows:

- *Percentage (contingent fee)*: The agent takes a percentage of the total dollar value of the contract.

- *Time*: The agent, typically an attorney, charges an hourly rate (usually $75 to $200) for each hour he spends working for the player.

- *Flat fee*: The agent agrees to negotiate the contract in return for a predetermined fee regardless of the time spent or the amount of the contract.

- *Combination*: The agent considers the time he spent and what he accomplished and then limits his fee to a maximum of 3, 4, or 5 percent of the contract's dollar value. One attorney-agent elaborated on the vague concept of "what was accomplished": "It depends on the context in which the player finds himself and the degree of success. There are some contracts that you know you've done an incredibly good job for the player."

The relative merits of each method of fee calculation are disputed by reputable agents and others in the field. The most widely criticized but most popular method is the percentage. Since most players already have a job and a prior year's salary as a starting point (or, for a rookie, at least the minimum salary), the agent's primary job is to negotiate an increase in the salary. For this reason some critics of the percentage method suggest that a contingent fee would reflect more closely the agent's performance if the fee were calculated as a percentage of the *increase* over the present contract. For example, if a player earning $100,000 signs a new contract for $150,000, the agent would collect a percentage of the $50,000 increase rather than of the $150,000 total.

The percentage method may encourage an unethical agent to place his immediate financial interests ahead of the player's overall interest. For example, the agent may be more inclined to seek a long-term contract when the athlete might be better served by proving himself under a shorter-term arrangement and then negotiating a new deal.

Proponents of the percentage system cite three advantages:

- There is a financial rather than a moral incentive for the agent to negotiate for more money;
- There is an incentive for the athlete to consult the agent more frequently since it will not cost him more as it would if the agent charged on a time basis;
- There is ease of financial calculation and accounting, particularly if the agent does more for the client than negotiate his contract.

After studying the various methods of fee calculation, the U.S. House of Representatives Select Committee on Professional Sports

> was unable to discern . . . that contingent fee arrangements were totally devoid of ethical value or that hourly or flat fees were pre-emptively superior. At best it could be said that contingent fee arrangements may be subject to greater abuse than, say, an agreed on flat rate, but that an hourly standard, favored by many because it has the benefit of allowing an agent to focus on the best overall bargain rather than the largest dollar package, is also open to abuse through the simple device of prolonging negotiations.

The athlete should discuss in detail an agent's method of fee calculation before agreeing to retain the agent. More than one player has discovered later that what he assumed to be free was not. After Greg Pruitt signed his first pro football contract, his agent reportedly gave him a list of every expense he had incurred while Pruitt was an undergraduate. The agent had insisted that if Pruitt needed anything, he should let him know, and Pruitt did.

If asked by an athlete, many agents will agree to an approximate total fee before the negotiations begin and will be willing to negotiate their fee. Regardless of how the agent calculates the fee, most reputable agents consider about 5 percent of the contract's value to be the maximum ethical fee. Some of the best agents charge about 3 percent. The fee may increase in unusual situations, such as to pay for additional specialized tax advice used in drafting the contract. An agent who provides services in addition to contract negotiation probably will charge an additional fee.

Finally, all compensation arrangements should be in writing, signed by the agent, even if there is no written representation agreement. At a minimum this document should specify:

- the services to be provided;
- the method and rate of charging for the services;
- how expenses will be handled;
- the frequency of billing and payment.

Question 13: When do I pay?

A few years ago an NFL rookie signed a $25,000 contract for two years with a $10,000 bonus. "That's a total of $60,000 and the agent took off his 10 percent, $6,000, right off the top," the president of the NFL Players Association told a reporter. "Well, the kid didn't make the team, so all he got to keep was the $4,000 left over from his bonus and the agent got to keep $6,000. That isn't fair."

Reputable agents agree: Fees should be collected as the player earns the compensation negotiated by the agent. The agent should not take a fee up front, in one payment, often taken out of the player's bonus. An even more outrageous practice occurs when an agent fails to obtain a guaranteed contract for his client, but cuts a deal with the team to guarantee the agent's 10 percent regardless of whether the player makes the team.

Up-front collection cheats a player in two ways. First, as the NFL rookie discovered, he may be cut and not receive part or all of the salary. Second, due to inflation, a dollar today buys more than today's dollar will buy next year and much more than today's dollar will buy in twenty years when the player may be collecting deferred compensation. But an agent who collects up front receives his entire fee in present dollars rather than in the inflated dollars the player will earn.

Consider this example: A player signs a ten-year contract for $2 million ($200,000 per year). His agent charges him a seemingly reasonable 5 percent fee, but collects the entire fee, $100,000, up front. "It's a gross misrepresentation to say his fee is 5 percent," Marvin Miller, executive director of the Major League Baseball Players Association told a reporter. "His fee is more like [50] percent of that player's first-year salary. It wouldn't be until after the tenth year that the agent's fee amounts to only 5 percent of the total package." For instance, one new baseball agent reportedly collected $330,000 in fees up front after negotiating a new multi-year contract for a client he obtained by buying the player's agency contract from his former agent.

Some agents add another twist to the up-front scam. They negotiate contracts with substantial portions of the salary deferred—paid later, usually after the player retires. In the worst cases, the agent takes his cut *up front* from the entire amount without adjusting for the effect of future inflation. He also takes credit publicly for negotiating seemingly high contracts.

One NFL executive told a reporter that it actually would cost his team only $226,000 to pay out a $1 million contract that is deferred over twenty years at $50,000 a year. Thus, both the team and the agent benefit at the expense of the player. While, under certain circumstances, deferring payment may be beneficial to an athlete, the athlete should insist that the agent's fee and time of collection be adjusted to reflect the true value of the deferred money.

It is reasonable for the agent to collect up front for his out-of-pocket expenses for the negotiations, such as telephone calls and airplane fares. The player should ascertain in advance whether or not such expenses are included in an agent's fee. In the case of athletes with reputations for not paying their bills, the agent may need to ensure that he will be paid for his services. But generally, an athlete should not pay an agent working on a percentage basis until the player receives the benefits of the agent's work.

Question 14: Should the agent collect his fee directly from the club?

Some agents prefer to collect their fees from the clubs rather than from the players. This can take two forms: Either the team actually pays the agent from its funds, or the team deducts the agent's fee from the player's paycheck and mails it to the agent. No reputable agent would accept the first situation. It raises serious questions about whether the agent is working for the team or the player. One agent explained:

> There's an inherent conflict in receiving his fee from the club. One would question for whom the agent is working. It's misleading to say, "listen, I'm going to get you a contract for X amount and the club will pay my fee." The player says, "OK, that's great."

Moreover, it may be more costly to the player, because the team will be paying him less if it also pays his agent. Major league baseball and the NBA have banned direct payment of an agent's fee by a team. Previously some NBA contracts provided for direct payment. Julius Erving's $2.96 million, six-year agreement through 1982 provided for a $60,000 payment to his agent. Paul Silas signed a $905,000 eight-year contract with provision for an $80,000 payment by the team to his agent. Direct payment may be appropriate for Canadian hockey players, because Canadian tax law, unlike U.S. tax law, does not allow the athlete to deduct agency fees from his income before calculating his tax obligation.

Some players prefer that the club deduct a portion of their salary from each paycheck and mail it to their agent. Responsible agents who favor this form of direct payment agree that the arrangement must be fully disclosed to the athlete in advance. The athlete should send a letter of instruction to the team, requesting that it send the agent a certain percentage of each of his paychecks. The letter should be valid only until revoked in writing by the player. The athlete's ability to stop payment to the agent—whether by withholding checks or by directing his team to stop the direct payment process—gives him some leverage and control over the agent. If the agent neglects his duties, the athlete can threaten to stop paying him.

Like the method of calculating the agent's fee and the timing of payment, whether or not the team should deduct the agent's fee from the player's paycheck is a matter which the player should discuss with the agent before making a decision. In no case should the player allow his agent to negotiate with the team the amount of the fee or any guarantees relating to the amount of the fee.

IV
Conflict—The Agent's Other Interests

Question 15: How might a club influence my relationship with my agent?
Question 16: How can the agent's other clients affect my interests?
Question 17: What does disclosure do for me?

Question 15: How might a club influence my relationship with my agent?

Teams sometimes have tried to co-opt an agent or otherwise reduce his usefulness to his clients. Some techniques, such as bribes or other payoffs, are outrageous abuses by the team and the agent. Other, more widely used techniques are more subtle and, perhaps, are legitimate business tactics.

A simple case illustrates why bribes have appealed to a few teams and agents. Suppose a team and an agent are $10,000 apart. The team offers to pass the agent $2,000 under the table if he will accept its salary offer. The team and agent will both be tempted. Both would benefit. Even if the agent charges a 10 percent fee, he still would collect only $1,000 if the player got the additional $10,000. The team saves $8,000. Only the player loses.

While cash bribes from teams to agents apparently are rare now, the situation differed during the early 1970s at the height of the war between the NBA and the American Basketball Association. "There were loads of stories of people who took cash to close deals," a basketball lawyer-agent said. "Statistically it was the single biggest abuse [by agents]."

Richard Sorkin testified about a more refined form of double-dealing. He told a New York State Senate committee that an owner of the St. Louis Blues had paid him $20,000 "in return for which Sorkin would 'give him first crack' at players he represented who were drafted jointly by the Blues and a member team of the World Hockey Association." The owner confirmed the payment, but said he had paid Sorkin for "scouting" young players.

The agent and his client may both be victims of various techniques sometimes used by clubs seeking to destroy a player-agent relationship. The club may seek to deal directly with the player or with another agent more amenable to the club's interests. Some clubs try to influence an agent by nurturing a friendly relationship with the agent. This approach may be both legitimate and more dangerous to the player than any outright abuse. It can be more difficult to recognize the harm done to a player by an agent who seems competent and honest, but who does not bargain hard enough because of the subtle way in which club officials have cultivated a cozy relationship with him.

Rather than attempt to influence a player's agent, club officials sometimes attempt to influence the player to fire the particular agent. An attorney-agent elaborated on one method formerly used by some basketball clubs:

> Some agents had very tight relationships with particular general managers. A general manager would break his ass to get another agent thown out and [his friend hired]. For example, he would offer a kid a really bad contract. It would not be long before somebody says, "you've got a bad agent. You should get somebody else."

A few professional teams may still attempt to destroy a player's relationship with his agent. One NFL team supposedly telephoned a kicker's parents and girl friend to criticize his agent and even asked alumni of the kicker's college to write to him and suggest that he find a new agent, according to the agent's law partner. When another team told a player that it would not meet his demands unless he fired this same agent, the agent told the player to "go in and take it." "He just walked in alone and signed the same contract." In a third case, "the club told the player, 'do you know he also represents so and so (who plays the same position)? How can he do the best job for you?'"

While these incidents show that a few clubs will still seek to pry a player away from an aggressive agent, most clubs will deal with whatever agent the player chooses. But the problem of management interference with the player-agent relationship has not disappeared; it has merely changed its form. A baseball lawyer-agent explained:

> In the past the goal was to deal with players representing themselves. The emphasis now is more on getting along with the agent, nurturing a relationship with the agent.

As an example of this sort of situation, he cited a prominent agent who believes that he should not try to squeeze every possible concession from the club without first weighing the interests of the club, the league, and even the fans. "[He] principally loves to be invited to management dinners and sit in owners' boxes." This agent, whose background as a labor lawyer leads him to conclude that it is wrong to accept anything from management, even a pen, espouses one viewpoint on the way an agent should deal with the club. To some degree this is more a matter of tactics than ethics. Some agents feel they can do a better job if they know the club officials on a more informal basis, even if it means sitting in their boxes. John Claiborne, former baseball executive, discussed the question from a management perspective:

> I have a pretty good rapport with most agents. . . . I leave them tickets. Some consider it a conflict, which is fine. Sometimes on a pretty full date they call for tickets and buy them. I can get too close to an agent. If I do too many favors, the players are going to wonder, "is this guy selling me down the river?"

Unlike double-dealing or trying to force out a particular agent, nurturing a cozy relationship with an agent through small favors is a legitimate business tactic. The athlete should discuss with a prospective agent his general approach to dealing with management. The athlete then can evaluate whether he will feel more comfortable with an agent who takes a hardline, adversarial tack or one who is more inclined to view his client's interests within a broader framework of the club's and even the sport's interest. Neither approach, or one in between, is necessarily the right one. In all cases, the player should make it clear to his agent that he expects the agent to put his client's interest ahead of his own relationship with the club.

A recent situation in baseball illustrates that some agents will sacrifice the interests of particular clients. Lawyers for the players' association found that many agents of recently traded players had not asked the players' old clubs for money owed to them under a baseball rule which entitles traded players to collect immediately all bonuses that hinge on future performance. One of the association lawyers involved noted:

> The overwhelming reaction was "the player didn't earn it; if I go in to the team, I'm going to look bad and hurt my relationship with the team." They're worried about other players or losing referrals from club officials.

If the player agrees with his agent that he is better off not asking for money owed to him, then it is the player's prerogative not to ask for it. But unless his agent informs him of his right to collect the money, the agent is neglecting his duty.

If the player's agent fails to inform the player of his rights for fear of jeopardizing the agent's relationship with the club, the old club certainly will not tell the player that he is entitled to more money. Neither can nor should the player expect the club to tell him that his agent is inept or dishonest. The adversarial nature of the negotiations process makes it extremely difficult and awkward for the club to make a fair assessment of whether the agent is abusing his fiduciary duty to the player. Michael Burke, president of the New York Knicks for nearly a decade, considered it "an untenable position" for the club to tell the player that his agent is no good. Burke believed that the most the club can do is advise the athlete in a "discrete" way that he may be better off if someone else represented him.

Before retaining an agent, an athlete should determine

whether that particular agent's approach to dealing with management suits the athlete's needs and standards. Other clients (and former clients) of the agent, the players' association, and sportswriters may be useful sources of information about the agent's relationship with management. An athlete should question the agent in depth about his tactical tools and ethical guidelines. While usually there is no single correct answer to questions about ethics, an athlete might find it useful to explore how an agent thinks about such questions and how he has put his thoughts into practice. A few sample questions:

- Do you accept free tickets and other favors from owners or general managers?
- When you represent two athletes drafted by the same team, do you try to finalize contracts for both before either signs?
- How do you feel about taking a client to a negotiating session?
- Under what circumstances would you suggest to a client that he find another agent?
- When do you feel that demanding renegotiation of a contract is justified?
- When do you advise your clients to withhold their services while under contract?

In summary, the player may be aided by his players' association, by published articles, or by other players in monitoring his agent's relationship with the club. But the player should realize that he himself maintains primary responsibility for protecting his own interests. The player should not hesitate to question his agent about his tactics and ethics in dealing with club officials.

Question 16: How can the agent's other clients affect my interests?

Most agents represent more than one client. Since a player often recommends his agent to teammates, three or four agents may represent the majority of players on a team. Occasionally such multiple representation creates problems for one of the players. For example, will the agent be less hard-nosed in negotiating any particular contract in order to cultivate the goodwill of the owner for his other clients and himself? If he represents two players who play the same position, will he play favorites? Will he even realize he is favoring one client over another?

While many of the situations conjured up in the area of conflicts of interest are "potential" or "hypothetical," *The Sporting News* reported on an actual problem involving two Kansas City Royals before the 1981 season. The agent who represented Hal McRae and Frank White refused to settle on White's contract until the Royals agreed to extend McRae's agreement, which had two years left. Royal management asserted that White, who had only one year left on his contract, could have signed a new contract a month earlier if his agent had tried to negotiate.

"I don't think he can use me as leverage to get Hal McRae a contract," White was quoted as saying. "[The agent] said he was going to do Hal's first, but if he has a roadblock there, I don't think he should hold me up." The agent reportedly responded to White's request to go ahead with his contract by saying he'd think about it.

"If your agent declines to come in and talk, you're going to have to give him an ultimatum," White said. "I'm ready to talk. I really don't want to go to spring training worrying about my contract."

An agent who represents several players on the same team will earn more money for some of those players (and for himself), but not necessarily for all of them. Each player should try to determine if he would be better off with a different agent. For example, a high-round football draft pick may suffer if his agent refuses to agree to terms offered until the team sweetens its offer to a lower-round pick whom the agent also represents.

The agent should have used his leverage to get a better offer for the high-round rookie. And it may work the other way—if, for example, an agent accepts less money for a utility infielder because the club buys an expensive car as the final inducement for a star's signature. Or what if the general manager tells the agent, "we can offer only one guaranteed contract and one no-trade contract to the seven players you represent"?

A few agents, according to a major league baseball player, are more concerned with collecting their fees than with negotiating the best possible contracts for their clients. These men go in to a general manager with set amounts for *their* fees in mind. If necessary, to get their desired cut, they may accept more money for one client and less for another even though the second client could have gotten a better contract.

In each of these situations, the players involved should consider whether or not the agent will be capable of passing this test: Can the agent separate and carry out his functions as if each of his clients was represented by a different agent?

Sometimes multiple representation on the same team can benefit the players. One agent may get more money in total for several players than the club would agree to pay if each player were represented by a different agent, according to two baseball executives, John Claiborne and Cedric Tallis. For example, five players who are represented by the same agent may sign contracts worth a total of $500,000. But if the same players each had a different agent, their contracts might be worth only $450,000. Claiborne explained that the agent may not actually play one player off against another; instead, the agent may use his representation of several players implicitly by arguing "you gave Smith a $10,000 raise and Jones $15,000, why shouldn't Brown get that much?"

When Congress investigated professional sports in 1976, it asked baseball agent Jerry Kapstein how he would respond if two outstanding rookie prospects, both competing for the third base job on the same team, came to him:

MR. SISK [chairman]. The point I am trying to make is are there times when you find yourself in a bit of a bind in negotiating the best possible contract for either or both of those individuals?

MR. KAPSTEIN. I have never been in that situation. . . . But I have not had any problems in Cincinnati [where] five of my clients are pitchers . . . [T]hey all work together for the benefit of the ball club. . . . I think competition among each individual is good. . . . There is no conflict of interest.

MR. ROSENBERG [committee counsel]. Suppose you had 10 players on a club and the general manager came to you and said, "Hey, I will settle for X dollars with four or five of these guys if you will give me a break on a couple of these others and take such and such so I can balance my books a little better this year."

Overall, if you did what he said, the club would save a few thousand dollars. If you hard bargain for every one of them and it would take you a very long time and you might get into a no-sign situation. . . .

MR. KAPSTEIN. I would say that never has come up with me. I am sure the clubs wish it had . . . I think they know me well enough that if they ever said that to me, my response would be an appropriate one . . . Each one is signed as an individual thing.

The give and take between Kapstein and the congressional committee indicates that there are few clear-cut, indisputable answers to difficult questions of possible conflict of interest. Conflict questions more often turn on philosophy than honesty. That is why it is so important for an athlete to be familiar and comfortable with his agent's attitude and approach.

A related concern is whether an agent has enough time to serve all his clients. Marvin Miller told a congressional committee studying the role of agents:

Some [agents] have bitten off more than they can chew. . . . Most players' contracts are being negotiated at about the same time with the clubs, and if you represent a couple of dozen players scattered from Texas to Montreal, and from New York to California, it is sometimes physically impossible to do justice to each of your clients.

As the committee noted in its final report, "much depends on the ability and resources of the individual agent." Since few, if any, agent are likely to admit to a lack of time, the player must make his own assessment and weigh it as one factor in his choice of agents. To protect himself against the possibility that the agent will not devote enough time to his interests, a player may want to include a clause in his agreement with his agent that such neglect will be cause for ending their relationship. Of course any agent—whether he represents one athlete or fifty—will have other demands on his time.

Players sometimes expect too much from their agents. Bob Woolf, in his book *Behind Closed Doors*, told of the day hockey player Derek Sanderson made four telephone calls from Honolulu to Boston before he reached Woolf. Sanderson's hotel room in Honolulu had no hot water, and he wanted his agent to complain to the manager.

Question 17: What does disclosure do for me?

All reputable agents agree that they would "disclose" any possible conflicts to the clients involved. Disclosure should mean a full and clear explanation. Unfortunately, this does not always happen. It is the player's responsibility to question the agent closely to try to understand how the conflict may affect his own interests and to determine whether the agent is treating him fairly.

In some cases, the player may want to accompany his agent to crucial negotiating sessions, in part to force the team to deal with him as an individual rather than as one of a group represented by the same agent. A successful baseball and football lawyer-agent, speaking at an ARPA meeting, listed three reasons why he sometimes takes a client to a crucial negotiating session:

- It shows the client that his agent is performing; he sees he is getting his money's worth and that he is represented by an agent who won't "wilt."
- It helps the athlete understand the situation.
- The team can see that the player is allied with his agent.

At the time the agent spoke he was negotiating a new contract with the Houston Astros for pitcher Vern Ruhle. The agent said he took Ruhle to a key meeting with Houston management in part because the general manager privately had told Ruhle, "Nothing personal, but you've been hurt by your agent." Ruhle subsequently signed an Astros contract reported to be worth at least $1.5 million for three years.

Other agents at the ARPA meeting said they preferred not to take their clients, in part because they felt they could bargain harder and cut a better deal if the general manager did not have the ability to face the athlete directly. Another agent believes that taking a player to the negotiations does not further the negotiation process. Instead, he believes that the agent who takes the player to negotiations does so only to cement his relationship with the player.

The possibility of a conflict may suddenly become more likely as a result of changes in the athlete's situation or the agent's practice. For example, due to several trades during a recent basketball season, one agent found himself representing a number of players on the New York Knicks. Afterwards, he observed:

> I didn't have any problem with the team. But a lot of problems arose with my clients, especially the guy who might get cut. The problem was more attorney-client. It was not an ethical problem.
>
> The end result of representing others might be to hurt [another client] in his job. The only thing you can do is to tell him you'll do the best for each.
>
> You can't structure who you accept as clients or you'd be forever hiring and firing clients. Most pros understand it, but don't like it.

Conflict—The Agent's Other Interests

Consider another possible conflict of interest situation: An agent represents two free agent all-star outfielders, Green and Black. Each knows the other retains the same agent. Both would like to play for the Sox. The Sox draft both, sign Green, and a week later sign Black. Then the Sox manager announces that he plans to use Green primarily as a designated hitter, while Black will fill the Sox outfield vacancy. But Green did not become a free agent in order to become a designated hitter. Should he blame his agent?

A common response to this type of situation from agents includes two elements: First, the agent should discuss the situation with each client. Second, as one agent told a columnist, "I don't choose, the ball clubs choose. I don't set the priorities, the ball clubs do." Another agent put it differently. "I don't think representation will affect the ultimate choice."

Since the agent will influence his client's choice, one way to analyze this situation is to consider what might have happened if the players had retained separate agents. Green's agent at least will ask the Sox about their interest in Black and the chances of signing him after they sign Green. Then the agent will discuss the situation with his client. If Green then signs with the Sox, hoping that the team won't sign Black, whatever happens is beyond the control of either the player or his agent.

However, if both players have the same agent, the agent will have a better sense of the prospects of Black joining the Sox. More significantly, the agent will influence which team Black chooses. This could harm Black if, in any way (perhaps even subconsciously), a desire to protect Green's interest influences the agent to guide Black to another team. Alternatively, the agent could reason that he did his best for Green, and now he'll do the same for Black even if it means Green winds up as a designated hitter.

This scenario obviously oversimplifies a complex situation. But like the dilemma the agent confronted in representing several players on the same basketball team, the free agent example illustrates that potential conflict of interest situations cannot be resolved by any general rules or guidelines.

If the agent is a practicing lawyer, he is bound by the lawyer's code of professional responsibility to disclose fully any conflict of interest to each client involved. But regardless of whether the agent is a lawyer, disclosure is only the first step. Understanding the subtle ramifications of a conflict situation is equally important. A player might find a third perspective from an uninvolved person helpful. This might be a trusted coach, a lawyer experienced in dealing with conflicts of interest in nonsports situations, or possibly a member of the players' association legal staff.

Unless the agent chooses to disqualify himself, the final decision and responsibility for the consequences rests with the athlete. Remember the test: Can the agent separate and carry out his functions as if all his clients were represented by different agents? In other words, is he treating each client fairly?

V
The Agent and His Principles

Question 18: What if I want to renegotiate my contract?

Question 18: What if I want to renegotiate my contract?

In 1980 Sam Cunningham demanded that the New England Patriots renegotiate his contract. The team refused, and Cunningham sat out the entire season. Before the next season his agent negotiated a substantial two-year contract with the Patriots. Whether or not Cunningham and several other players who sat out a season succeeded financially is debatable.

One player who benefitted financially by staying out of training camp even though his contract had a year to go was pitcher Doyle Alexander. On the eve of the 1982 season the Giants traded Alexander to the Yankees, and he signed a new contract.

Infielder Lenny Randle announced his retirement from baseball one February because the New York Mets would not renegotiate the five-year contract he had signed a season earlier. Forty-eight hours later "Randle changed his mind after his agent reminded him of 'the sanctity of the contract, even a bad one.'"

As Randle was informed, when a player signs a contract he legally binds himself to perform to the best of his ability for the length of the contract according to the terms of the contract. In return, the team pays him a salary and benefits. But nothing (short of a clause in the contract forbidding discussion of renegotiation) prevents a player from asking to renegotiate before the contract expires. And nothing compels the club to agree. One commercial attorney who also represents several baseball players observed:

> I don't see anything unethical about a player or agent coming in and saying, based on these factors the player should be given an extension, a bonus, or a higher salary. It would be unethical for the player or agent to threaten some action. In the commercial world contracts are renegotiated on a daily basis. It's certainly a questionable practice, but the problem is that it may be justified.

A large sports management firm states its policy more bluntly: Renegotiation is justified when the client wants his contract renegotiated and if the client has some element of leverage to use in the renegotiation.

A player, his agent, or both may feel that the player deserves to have his contract renegotiated in at least three situations:

(A) Outstanding performance well beyond expectations;
(B) Gross unfairness in the original bargaining situation;
(C) Disagreement stemming from unwritten promises.

A. Outstanding performance well beyond expectations

On his nineteenth birthday, Wayne Gretzky signed a multimillion-dollar 21-year personal services contract with Peter Pocklington, owner of the Edmonton Oilers. Within two years Gretzky had established himself, not just as a young potential superstar but as one of the greatest players and biggest drawing cards in National Hockey League history. Midway through the 1981–82 season, Gretzky signed a new contract with Pocklington and the Oilers, one that reportedly would increase his compensation to nearly one million dollars annually and be worth as much as twenty million dollars over 21 years.

When a player performs well beyond the team's expectations at the time he signed a multiyear contract—especially if his salary is less than that of teammates of similar talent—the club may want to renegotiate the terms of the contract or negotiate an extension. "The club wants people who are happy, not feeling victimized," said one attorney-agent, citing his extensive discussions with the Dodgers about Ron Cey's contract. Michael Burke offered a management perspective:

> If a youngster like Ron Guidry had signed a three-year contract at $22,000 a year and had the kind of year he had [in 1977] and the Series he had for the Yankees, it would be a foolish club who wouldn't tear up his contract. But if a guy who makes $300,000 suddenly says, "I want $500,000," I don't think that is justified.

Rather than "renegotiate" Guidry's contract, the Yankees signed him to an extended contract. "I don't even like to consider renegotiation," said Cedric Tallis, then the Yankee general manager. Four years later, after testing the free agent market, Guidry's agent negotiated a new contract with the Yankees, reportedly for at least $3 million over four years.

Sometimes the team's motives in offering a new contract are less honorable. For example, some football teams have asked a player to negotiate a new contract just *before* the coach tells the player he's going to start his first game. An astute agent will help the player recognize this ploy and negotiate accordingly.

B. Gross unfairness in the original bargaining situation

A fifth-round draft choice signed a multiyear agreement with the New York Jets negotiated by his coach. As a fifth-round choice he had little leverage, so he accepted a long-term contract at little more than the minimum salary. But he earned a starting job during his rookie season. The next summer he called a press conference to announce that he would leave training camp unless the Jets agreed to renegotiate his contract. He got a new contract.

Some agents who generally oppose such tactics to obtain a new contract would make an exception in this type of situation. One agent explained, "the club won't offer a one-year deal. If they would, then there would be no need to worry about renegotiating. But the situation is different when they're cramming down long-term contracts." He believes the situation is fairer in baseball, where one-year contracts are standard for young, unproven players.

Another agent, commenting on a similar situation, concluded that he would not renegotiate if the athlete was "properly represented" and, in his opinion, offered "the semblance of a fair deal." But "proper" representation and "semblance" of a "fair deal" are subjective criteria, as one agent's highly publicized attempt to renegotiate the contracts of two new England Patriots, John Hanna and Leon Gray, illustrates. Each previously had a different agent, but both were "just so manifestly underpaid" and had not received additional compensation promised orally, according to a law partner of their new agent. Nevertheless, after each player sat out several games in futile support of their demands, an NFL player-management committee met for eight hours and then ordered both players to fulfill their contractual commitments.

Sometimes a player insists on renegotiating his contract even though his team *and* his agent refuse. Julius Erving's first agent recalled Doctor J's demand to renegotiate his guaranteed four-year, $125,000 annual contract with the Virginia Squires after his outstanding rookie season:

> I refused to do so and asked him if he had had a terrible year if he would have returned $25,000. He replied, "Of course not." He didn't see the point and renegotiated the contract with a new representative.

While this agent has proposed the barring of oral promises and renegotiating, except when allowed by a specific clause in a contract, many agents view the opportunity to reopen a long-term contract as beneficial to the player and the club. Erving's second agent has asserted that he often obtains a club's oral agreement to renegotiate a written contract later to take into account the player's proven performance and drawing ability. "When I have represented a player in renegotiating his contract, team representatives have almost always honored their oral agreements to renegotiate the contracts and have dealt with me in good faith," the agent wrote in *The New York Times*.

C. *Disagreement stemming from unwritten promises*

When Philadelphia Phillies shortstop Larry Bowa discovered that management does not always honor oral promises, he was "burning." Near the end of the 1981 season, Bowa, with one year remaining on his contract, told the Phillies owner, Ruly Carpenter, that he wanted either a new three-year contract or to be traded. Carpenter reportedly agreed and noted their discussion in writing for the Phillies' files. But Carpenter sold the team soon after the end of the season and the new management, which may have been unaware of the alleged oral understanding, refused to honor the agreement. Bowa, according to news reports, was "burning." He told a *Sporting News* reporter, "This hurts me more than anything I've been through. I've been with an organization that has been dead honest with me. Now, all of a sudden, all I get is deceit, lies." The Phils later traded Bowa to the Cubs, and he signed a three-year contract at a reported $500,000 a year.

Pitcher Skip Lockwood explained to a sportswriter how a typical unwritten promise problem is created:

> The player asks what happens if he has a good year after he signs. They wink and say, "Sure, come in and we'll open the contract." A problem is born.

Any promises not contained in the player's written contract may produce considerable misunderstanding and hard feelings. The player is in an awkward position for two reasons: First, the oral promises may violate the rules of the sport (at least in baseball) or be legally unenforceable or both. Second, the player's rights in the dispute may only be moral ones and, as such, a matter of opinion. The player's teammates, the press, and fans may also disagree with his stance, making life uncomfortable for the athlete and his family and potentially reducing his attractiveness for endorsements and appearances.

Consider the case of then Boston pitcher Luis Tiant as an example of the problem that Lockwood identified. After winning 21 games in 1976, Tiant wanted to renegotiate the two-year contract he had signed with the Red Sox after holding out the previous spring. He disagreed with the club's interpretation of an oral bonus and guarantee provision negotiated by Tiant, his agent, and the Red Sox owner, Thomas Yawkey, in March 1976. Yawkey's death in July 1976 complicated the situation:

Yawkey allegedly had promised orally to guarantee the contract for both 1976 and 1977.

By March 1977 the Red Sox had agreed to guarantee the contract for 1977, but Tiant was still not satisfied. Incensed at the club's earlier refusal to live up to his understanding of the 1976 agreement with Yawkey, Tiant demanded a guaranteed contract for 1978 at a modest salary increase. While his agent negotiated with the club in Florida, Tiant remained at home near Boston rather than report to training camp as his agent urged him to do.

Both sides finally agreed in mid-March to leave unchanged the terms of Tiant's 1977 contract but to extend the contract for one year—guaranteed, with a $25,000 raise. Tiant reported to training camp about three weeks late and compiled a disappointing 12–8 record for the season. After the 1978 season Tiant (represented by another agent) became a free agent and signed a two-year contract with the Yankees.

In retrospect, former Red Sox executive John Claiborne believes it was worth taking the risk that Tiant would not pitch as well early in the season in order to establish a firm no renegotiation policy:

> It's a bad decision to renegotiate any time, particularly now with multi-year contracts. If you do that for one player, you'll have 24 others lining up expecting it to be done for them.

Former pitcher Sam McDowell parlayed a disagreement over a side letter into a trade from the light-hitting Cleveland Indians to the then potent San Francisco Giants. His last contract with the Indians contained a performance clause depending on the number of games he won. But such "performance clauses" were not permitted in major league baseball rules. So, the Indians' obligation to pay the bonus was expressed in a side letter.

After newspaper reports about performance clauses in several contracts, the Commissioner of Baseball decided to nullify the bonus provisions. He sent a letter to McDowell telling him that the letter agreement was null and void. McDowell took the letter to his agent, who told him that the letter presented Sam with the possibility that the Commissioner's letter had caused the Cleveland Indians to breach his contract. The agent further advised McDowell to immediately commence a "holdout." McDowell sat down and began an intense negotiation with the Indians. As a result, McDowell returned to the team, but his agent had secured an oral promise (from owner Gabe Paul) that McDowell would be traded when the season was over—and he was traded, to the Giants for Gaylord Perry.

Situations such as those of McDowell, Bowa, Tiant, and Randle—who "felt there was 'a spiritual violation [by the Mets] of a moral agreement'"—illustrate an important point: The player, his agent, and management must try to make certain that each party clearly understands the precise terms—written and oral—of the agreement between the club and the player. Anything not written as part of the contract usually will not be legally enforceable.

The decision on whether to rely on anything other than the terms of a written contract involves a number of factors, some of which vary from sport to sport. These factors include the player's present bargaining power and how much it is likely to change in the next few years, the regulations in the sport about bonuses and oral promises, the character of the responsible club officials, and the agent's past arrangements with particular officials. There are other factors, beyond the player's control, such as injuries or trades or, as Bowa discovered, sale of the team.

A Matter of Individual Judgment

On January 13, 1982, *The New York Times* reported that Chicago Cubs first baseman Bill Buckner was threatening to sit out the 1982 season unless his contract was extended or renegotiated. The contract had three years to run at $310,000.

The story quoted Buckner:

> I hate to sound like a crybaby. Three hundred thousand dollars is a lot of money. But you have to go by what your equals are getting. I know if I'd been a free agent I'd have gotten what Ken Griffey got from the Yankees. But I wasn't a free agent. Besides, I don't want that much money. I'm just asking for an extension.

That same week *The Sporting News*, in a feature story on Seattle Supersonics center Jack Sikma, noted that Sikma recently had signed a three-year extension of his contract for $1.2 million per year. "Until this year, Sikma had been an all-star player receiving bench warmer wages at $180,000 a season, but he never complained, threatened to sit out or asked for his contract to be renegotiated," the story stated before quoting Sikma's explanation:

> "I just felt comfortable doing it the way I did. I maybe could have renegotiated, but when you do that, you are extending your contract and tying yourself into more years. I made a deal and I wasn't doing all that badly. A deal is a deal, and if I would have renegotiated a couple of years ago, my value then was probably only around $400,000 to $500,000 a year. I more than made up for that the way it turned out. I don't feel I sacrificed anything monetarily. An injury could have meant a sacrifice, but I've been lucky, I guess."

The final decision as to whether to renegotiate, what tactics to use, and how far to carry those tactics is a matter of individual judgment by the athlete, his agent, and other advisers. Since successful renegotiation will usually result in a longer-term contract, the player must make economic as well as ethical calculations. Factors relating to how his bargaining power is likely to change over the life of his present contract and the risk of injury must be addressed.

Once again, before signing with an agent, the athlete should discuss his situation in detail with that agent. He should ask the agent about his ethics and tactics concerning oral promises and renegotiation. One controversial football and basketball agent described his approach to a reporter for *The New York Times*:

> In every situation—going into camp, not going into camp, signing, not signing, how much money—I try to present every alternative and the probabilities of it. . . . I never tell a young man "walk out, stay in, sign, don't sign."

The way an agent presents a situation will often influence a client's decision. A player may be able to determine whether an agent favors "withholding services" by asking him how many of his clients have held out for renegotiation by not reporting to training camp and for how long they stayed out. Moreover, an agent's attitude toward threatening not to report and actually not reporting may provide one indication of the agent's philosophy of representation.

In summary, a player pondering an attempt to renegotiate his contract should consider these points:

- Management often will be willing to discuss renegotiating or at least extending the present contract if the player continues to abide by his contract during the negotiations. Many contracts are quietly renegotiated or extended.
- If the owner will not discuss any contractual changes, the player has a choice of complying with his contract or walking out. Such action may be costly to the player financially (in fines), performance-wise, or both, and may violate his legal obligations to the owner of the team. However, it may result in a substantial raise or a trade to a team that is more inclined to negotiate a new contract.
- If the team has violated a term of the contract, refusing to practice or play may be necessary to protect the player's legal rights and to force a resolution of the dispute. In this situation a player may need the assistance of his union as well as his agent, and possibly an attorney.

- A player may be able to avoid any renegotiation problems by retaining a competent and honest agent and making sure that all management promises are written into the contract. One term of the contract might be an agreement to reopen the contract at a given point or under certain circumstances. The player and his agent should make their own written notes of anything that is not written into the contract.

- If the agent refuses to renegotiate, the player may have to seek a new agent (if he is not bound by contract to the present agent). This could be a major disruption for the athlete and his family, especially if he had enjoyed a relationship of trust and confidence with his agent.

- The final decision is the player's. A good agent will use his expertise and experience to outline the player's options and their likely consequences. But the athlete has to live with the results—financial, psychological, moral, and legal.

VI
Regulation

Question 19: Who regulates agents?
Question 20: What role do players' associations play?

Question 19: Who regulates agents?

After playing thirteen years in the NBA, Rudy Tomjanovich said, "I thought things were getting better but now it seems there are a lot of underhanded guys out there."

A counsel to the Major League Baseball Players Association for more than ten years thought he had heard about most of the abuses worked by agents against baseball players. But after he had resigned as counsel and started representing players, he said, "If anything has come across, it's more frightening and there are more improper courses of conduct than I imagined."

This attorney cited as an example of an "outrageous agent" a man with a religious name who tells players, "I'm not one, I just changed my name for business reasons.' He calls reporters, says he represents certain players whom he doesn't represent, and gets stories as advertisements." The attorney labeled this agent a "destructive force" and predicted that even though many other players know about his reputation, "he will still get away with it."

So, who regulates agents? Essentially, no one.

Various entities are trying to regulate some agents, or at least reduce the incidence of incompetency, dishonesty, and deception, but none has succeeded. The role of one major force, the players' associations, is discussed in the next section. A discussion of five other possible sources of regulation and the reasons none has the authority or ability to regulate all agents on a comprehensive basis follows.

The Association of Representatives of Professional Athletes

ARPA was founded in 1978 with the aid of the National Football League Players Association. Now independent, ARPA's membership includes experienced and well-regarded agents as well as prospective agents with varying qualifications. The Association seeks to improve the competency of agents by offering educational seminars and to improve the ethical standards of the profession through its code of ethics. ARPA publishes an annual directory of its members with a summary of their qualifications. Its 1982 directory listed 69 members. Many highly regarded agents (and, undoubtedly, some unscrupulous agents) are not members of ARPA. *Washington Post* staff writer Bart Barnes, after noting that ARPA is trying to promote standards of competence, professionalism, and integrity, wrote: "But since membership is entirely voluntary, ARPA lacks clout, and no one in the business is forced to subscribe to its code of ethics unless he or she chooses."

ARPA reorganized in the fall of 1982. It plans to try to attract more members, especially the more prominent agents, and to publish a monthly newsletter.

Lawyers' organizations and state bar rules

Only agents who practice law are subject to the ethical rules and disciplinary procedures of the legal profession. Lawyers who are not admitted to the bar of the state in which their agency office is located, or who are not practicing law, generally do not consider themselves bound by the bar rules. Except in the most flagrant situations, such as criminal conviction, they can generally avoid the scrutiny of the bar system.

The American Bar Association (ABA) has formed a committee (open to any of its members) concerned with legal issues related to sports. Although the Sports Division of the ABA's Forum Committee on the Entertainment and Sports Industries seeks to educate lawyers about issues in athlete representation (among other topics), it is not set up to play a regulatory role. Neither is another lawyers' organization, the Sports Lawyers Association. It seeks to inform and educate its members about the legal affairs of pro athletes, teams, leagues, and sports games.

State Law

In September 1981, California became the first state to enact a law that specifically regulates sports agents. The California statute requires all agents (except any California lawyer when "acting as legal counsel") to register annually with the state, to pay a license fee, and to deposit a $10,000 surety bond. The State Labor Commission may investigate the moral character of any applicant and, upon proper notice and hearing, may refuse to grant a license or may suspend or revoke a license.

The agent must file a copy of the contracts he signs with athletes. To protect amateur athletes, the contract must state prominently that an athlete may jeopardize his or her amateur standing by signing the contract. As a disincentive to agents who induce student-athletes to violate the eligibility rules, the law requires an agent to file a copy of his registration statement with a student's school before contacting, *in any manner*, a student. Any contract made with a student must be filed with the school within five days or else it is void and unenforceable. Violation of the agent law carries a minimum $1,000 fine, 60 days imprisonment, or both.*

Whether agent regulation by only one state will improve the situation is unclear. Undoubtedly other states and groups with an interest in curbing the abuses worked by sports agents will carefully monitor the impact of the California law. The chairman of the New York State Senate Select Committee on Crime, after holding hearings in 1978 on the abuses committed by sports agents, concluded that legislation to control agents was needed. New York has yet to act, but a bill similar to the California law was under consideration in 1982.

Federal Regulation

Congress also has considered national regulation. In 1976, a congressional committee declared that the role of sports agents

---
*The text of the law is reprinted in Appendix F.

was a matter of federal concern and cited the regulation of farm labor contractors and stock brokers as precedents for federal intervention. The committee, however, called for further investigation and recommended that the players' associations, bar associations, and other interested parties pool informational resources and consider establishing uniform professional standards for agents. Its report concluded, "it is more likely that the onus of establishing and enforcing professional standards will be on the industry itself."

The Leagues
To a limited degree the leagues can reduce the possibility of an agent abusing his relationship with an athlete. Major league baseball, for example, requires that a player submit an agent authorization form before a team may negotiate with the agent. The Commissioner periodically notifies these registered agents of rules such as those which govern contacts between teams and potential free agents.* Although the notice warns that agents who violate these rules may be disqualified from future player representations, it is not clear how such a penalty would be enforced. Both baseball and the NBA bar direct payment of agent fees by teams.

The ability of the leagues to control agent depends in large part upon mutual agreement with the players' union. Some of the limitations on the unions in regulating agents are discussed in the next chapter.

The collective bargaining agreements between the players' associations and all major team sports assures each player of the right to assistance by a "representative of his choice" in negotiating his individual salary. Unless the players impose their own regulation scheme—a difficult proposition politically and legally—certain agents inevitably will escape regulation.

---

*The agent authorization form and a copy of a letter from the Commissioner to player agents are reprinted in Appendix E.

Even if there were a public or private regulatory authority, it would be difficult to determine meaningful workable requirements for licensing agents and even more difficult to ensure compliance.

Question 20: What role do players' associations play?

Outfielder Bobby Bonds signed what he and his agent thought was a guaranteed contract for more than $400,000 annually for four years. After two years, the St. Louis Cardinals released Bonds and refused to pay the approximately $880,000 remaining on the four-year contract which Bonds claimed they owed him. Since the contract omitted the specific language necessary to create a guarantee, the Cardinals contended full payment was required only if Bonds made the major league team.

Bonds turned to the Major League Baseball Players Association for help. The Association's legal staff began developing a case for Bonds based on the legal concept of mutual mistake—both sides intended to make the contract guaranteed and only inadvertently omitted the requisite language. As evidence of the parties' intent, Bonds could cite a section of the contract which specified exceptions to the nonexistent guarantee clause. The Association, as it does in all contract enforcement disputes, would pay all of Bond's legal expenses, including the cost of flying him to hearings. The Association's chief counsel, Donald Fehr, speaking at an ARPA seminar, cited the Bonds case as a prime example of "stupid mistakes" by a player's agent and as a problem which could have been avoided if the agent had asked the Association to review the contract before Bonds signed. Bonds eventually settled for $215,000.

The players' association in each team sport serves as exclusive bargaining agent for the players for almost all matters except individual compensation. The players vote to establish an association as their union and pay dues (deducted from their paychecks) to finance the union. An executive director, elected by the members, heads each association.

The relationship between the association and its members and the leagues is governed by federal labor law. The rights and obligations of the players, teams, and leagues are set forth in a document known as the collective bargaining agreement, sometimes referred to as the basic agreement. The agreements usually run for periods of three to eight years. The negotiations on new agreements have led to strikes in baseball and football and have been profoundly influenced by lawsuits in all sports.

Among the items typically (but not always) covered by the collective bargaining agreement are the following:

- Conditions under which a player has the ability to change teams as a free agent;
- Minimum salaries; maximum salary reduction;
- Grievance procedures;
- The uniform contract form,* to which only provisions which are not inconsistent may be added. (For example, in 1976 several Boston Red Sox players tried to sign contracts which, after the contract expired, would have given Boston the right to match any other team's contract offer and keep the player. The Players Association rejected the contracts because they were inconsistent with the free agent terms of the collective bargaining agreement.);
- Scheduling;
- Salary arbitration (particularly significant in baseball, where arbitration has enabled players not eligible for free agency to obtain substantial salary increases, and other players, by threatening to go to arbitration, to negotiate multiyear, guaranteed contracts);
- Expense allowances;
- Termination pay;
- Postseason playoff pay;

---

*For examples of uniform players' contracts, see Appendix D.

- Safety and health;
- Preseason training conditions;
- Transfers of players;
- Roster size;
- Amateur draft procedures;

Although the players' associations do not directly regulate agents, they informally counsel members (upon request) about their choice of agents and other advisers. They also help inform and educate agents, provide salary information, and work with agents in areas ranging from developing arbitration strategy to processing grievances. The involvement of the four major players' associations in these areas varies, as does the relationship between the associations and agents.

The executive directors of the hockey and basketball associations also privately represent athletes in their sports, while staff members of the baseball and football players' associations work solely for the associations. The basketball and hockey executive directors have repeatedly denied accusations that the dual role poses conflicts. Lawrence Fleisher, the NBA Players Association executive director since its inception in 1961, has stated that a conflict which hurt either the association or an individual client "has never been shown." He continued:

> There is a potential conflict of interest in everything we do. The association and the players know what I do. My interests are to get a maximum for everybody in the union.

By the time the NFL bargaining agreement expired on July 15, 1982, an increasing amount of bitterness had developed between many football agents and the NFL Players Association. The center of the dispute was the union's proposal for a wage scale for all players, a scheme that would significantly reduce the need for agents. In addition, the union offered 1982 draft choices contract advice from their team's player representative.

The football situation and the dual role of the basketball and hockey executive directors are among the explanations given for the associations' failure to take a more active role in regulating agents. Another difficulty is that until an athlete signs a contract with a major league team, he is not a member of the association. Two former counsels to players' associations reflected on the question of possible conflict between agents and the unions. Baseball's Richard Moss observed:

> A good question is what goes on in the players' minds? Do they separate the association and their individual representatives and feel that there's an inherent conflict (which is not true in reality)? Many perceive the players association as generally hostile to the whole thing. That's not so.

James Quinn, while working for the NBA Players Association, explained why he believed an informational rather than a regulatory role best served the association's membership:

> As a union, we're required to protect our members. We think players are intelligent enough that when given certain information, they can decide.

He suggested that word of mouth was generally effective to "sort out the bad apples" among agents.

The associations have considered compiling and possibly publishing a list of approved agents. Alan Eagleson, executive director of the National Hockey League Players' Association, explained one strong argument against a listing.

> The Players' Association is caught in a difficult position, in that we cannot approve or disapprove of individual agents without running the risk of a law suit by any agent who is not included in the approved list.

Another risk raised by publishing a list of approved agents is that a disgruntled player might try to hold the association responsible for the actions of a listed agent. Eagleson explained:

If problems exist, the player may say to the association, "you gave him the Good Housekeeping Seal of Approval; I'm looking to you for the money."

Besides their role in regard to agents and negotiating the collective bargaining agreement, the players' associations typically perform these functions:

- Negotiate and help administer the players' pension plan;
- Monitor enforcement of the collective bargaining agreement, including filing and supporting grievances and reviewing all contracts to be sure they conform with the terms of the agreement;
- Review and sometimes veto rule changes. (In 1980, the National Hockey League Players' Association, for example, vetoed the introduction of overtime periods.);
- Serve as the player's advocate in salary and other arbitration situations;
- Monitor injuries and study safety standards. (The NFL Players Association, for example, has been particularly active in investigating and complaining about dangers of artificial turf.);
- Inform and educate the players concerning their rights under the collective bargaining agreement and the issues under consideration in negotiating a new agreement;
- Act as agent for the members in selling certain rights, such as the rights to reproduce players' photos on bubble gum cards;
- Help facilitate responsible investments by players by arranging for financial advice through nationally recognized investment firms.

This is only a partial list. The role of each association varies by sport and evolves according to the needs and desires of its members. The appropriate role for each players' association in regulating agents (and in other matters) is one which each member athlete can influence. It is a subject for players to discuss with one another and with their advisers. Both the agent and the association work for the best interests of the athlete, but the agent serves the best interest of individual athletes while the association serves the best interests of all the players in that sport. These interests often are the same, but can be quite different.

Conclusion
The Athlete's Responsibility

If all players wanted agents who are bonded, licensed, bound by a code of ethics, educated in the current basic agreement and tax laws, and who are left-handed, over six feet tall, and red-haired, plenty of agents would appear who meet all those criteria. But first the players must let the agents know what they want and expect.

Any athlete before hiring an agent should ask about the agent's qualifications, ethics, philosophy of representation, approach to dealing with club owners, method of calculating and collecting his fees, attitude toward renegotiation, and anything else that matters to the player. Each athlete after retaining an agent should monitor the agent's performance, participate in making crucial decisions, and make sure the agent does not subordinate the player's interests to those of any other client.

If a player fulfills this responsibility, his relationship with his agent may be nearly as satisfying as Frank Tanana's; he chose his agent to be the best man at his wedding. If a player neglects his duty, his relationship with his agent may wind up as barren and bitter as Dennis Duval's tragic encounter with Richard Sorkin.

Glossary

Set forth below are some of the terms used in the book with a description of their meanings. The description is neither a legal nor a dictionary definition of the terms.

Agent: A professional sports agent acts on behalf of an athlete in negotiating the athlete's playing contract with a professional team or organization. Agents often perform additional services, ranging from helping the athlete supplement his income through speaking engagements and product endorsements to counseling the athlete about preparing for a career after his playing days are over.

Arbitration: A method of solving disputes in which each side submits a proposal and argues its case and an independent person or board makes a decision. It is commonly used in sports to settle disputes relating to the interpretation of contract terms.

ARPA: The Association of Representatives of Professional Athletes was founded in 1978 to improve the competency of agents by offering educational seminars and to improve the ethical standards of the profession.

Bonus: A sum of money paid to an athlete for signing a contract or meeting certain criteria, such as playing in a certain number of games or making an all-star team.

Client: The athlete is the agent's client.

Collective Bargaining Agreement: A document negotiated between the players' union and the owners in a particular league which sets forth the rights and obligations of the players, the teams, and the league. Also known as the basic agreement.

Commissioner: The head of each professional team sport. He is elected by a vote of the club owners.

Conflict of Interest: This term refers to a situation in which an agent faces competing demands by two or more of his clients. For example, if an agent represents the starting center on a basketball team, and another center, who is also his client, is traded to that team, the agent may face a conflict of interest in negotiating a new contract for either player.

Contract: A legal document which sets forth the obligations of two or more parties to each other. Usually one party agrees to pay the other party in return for his services.

Deferred Compensation: Money paid to a player some time after the year in which he performs services for that money. It may be paid during or after his playing career; it sometimes, but not always, includes interest on the original amount specified in a player's contract.

Disclosure: The act of notifying a client of certain information relevant to his relationship with the agent. For example, attorneys are required to disclose conflicts of interest to their clients.

Eligibility: This term refers to whether or not an athlete is qualified under NCAA and league rules to compete for a school. A college athlete usually has four seasons of eligibility in any sport.

Exclusive Contract: In relation to an agent, this refers to an arrangement whereby the agent is the only person authorized to represent the athlete. He may be able to claim his fee for any contracts entered into by the athlete even if the agent did not participate in the negotiations.

Fiduciary: This is the relationship between the agent and the athlete. It is an obligation of confidence and trust under which the agent is expected as a matter of law to work and act in the best interest of the athlete.

Financial Management: This covers the process of budgeting, paying bills, tax planning, and investing the athlete's money. Also known as financial planning. It requires experience, willingness to help an athlete define his financial goals, and the ability to relate investment and other recommendations to those goals.

Free Agent: An amateur athlete who has been passed over in a professional draft, or a veteran athlete whose contract has expired or who has been released from his contract.

Grievance: A dispute involving interpretation of, application of, or compliance with the provisions of a player's contract or the collective bargaining agreement. If the player and the club cannot resolve the dispute, it is usually settled by arbitration. Either the player or the club may file a grievance claim as provided for in the collective bargaining agreement.

Guaranteed Contract: A contract by which a player will be paid even if he fails to make the team. Terms of a guaranteed contract vary significantly and usually include exceptions, such as injuries resulting from participation in other sports or the player reporting out of shape. A contract may be partially guaranteed; for example, the salary for the first year only or part of the salary for each year may be guaranteed.

Long-Term Contract: A contract that extends for more than one year. The term is frequently used in football to refer to a series of one-year contracts signed at the same time.

Merchandising: Also known as a product endorsement, this term refers to lending an athlete's name or picture to promote a sale of a product.

Minimum Salary: The least amount that a player can be paid under the terms of the collective bargaining agreement.

NCAA: The National Collegiate Athletic Association, the governing body of college athletics.

No-Cut Contract: This term is often used interchangeably with guaranteed contract, although a true no-cut contract will assure the player of a spot on the major league team's roster.

Option Year: This term usually refers to the last year that a team may prevent a player from being a free agent. The terms of the contract for the option year and the circumstances in which they can be included in a player's contract vary from sport to sport.

Pension Plan: A system under which money is paid (usually by teams), into a fund from which retired players receive payments. Each sport has its own pension plan, and the criteria for qualifying for the pension (vesting), the amount of a payment, and the age at which a player may begin to receive the payments differ from sport to sport.

Player Representatives: In most sports the players on each team elect a teammate to represent them as part of that union governing board.

Players' Association: The players' union in a particular sport. The players pay dues to the union and elect an executive director as their union leader.

Power of Attorney: A document authorizing another person to perform certain acts or kinds of acts on behalf of the athlete. A power of attorney may be limited to a specific act or may be very broad.

Present Value: Refers to how much a given amount of money at a certain date in the future would be worth today. For example, the present value of $10,000 to be paid in 10 years, assuming an annual inflation rate of 12 percent, is about $3,030.

Principal: The person for whom the agent works. The athlete is the principal in the athlete-agent relationship.

Release: When a team cuts a player, it releases him from his contract. This may require the team to ask "waivers" from all other teams in the league; that is, for the other teams to pass on their right to claim the player.

Tax Return: The forms filed with the government to report a person's income and claim deductions from income. Most federal tax returns are due each year on April 15.

Tax Shelter: An investment that also provides tax advantages that may reduce the amount of income tax a person owes on his other income. In contrast to other investments, the after-tax return (benefit) is greater than the before-tax return. Athletes are offered many tax shelters that may be poor investments, or illegal, or both.

Uniform Contract: In the team sports most terms of a player's contract are standardized as a part of the collective bargaining agreement. Bonuses and salary are the major items not established as part of the uniform contract.

Up-Front Payment: Refers to the practice of some agents of collecting their fee when the player signs a long-term contract rather than collecting it in installments as the player receives the salary provided for by the contract.

Appendixes

A: The Professional Drafts

Each professional team sport holds an annual draft of amateur players. Baseball holds two drafts a year, and the North American Soccer League holds a primary draft and two supplemental drafts. The result of the draft is that only one team will negotiate with each athlete selected. If he does not sign a contract with that team, he may not play in the league until after the next draft. Except for football, all professional sports will draft athletes with college eligibility remaining as well as college seniors.

The teams make their selections in turn, starting with those teams who finished the previous season with the worst records and working up to the championship teams. Except in baseball, teams may trade their draft rights. Teams may also lose draft rights as compensation for signing free agents.

Set forth below is a sport-by-sport description of the draft process and rules.

Football

The basic rule in the NFL is that only college players who have completed their eligibility may be drafted. Loss of eligibility through withdrawal or dismissal from school or through signing of a professional contract in another football league (for example, a minor league) does *not* qualify a player for the draft.

A player who *graduates* before his eligibility expires may be drafted by declaring in writing to the NFL commissioner before April 15 his intent to be graduated before the fall semester. If the player is selected in the draft, the selecting team cannot offer a contract until the player's college has notified the NFL office of his graduation. If he fails to graduate, the selecting team loses the selection *and* the player loses his college eligibility. Players who took the graduation route to the NFL in 1982 included Michigan offensive tackle Ed Muransky and Penn State guard Mike Munchak.

A few players qualify for the draft through the *five-year rule*: a player can be drafted if five league seasons have elapsed since the player first entered, attended, practiced football at, or participated in football games for a recognized junior college, college, or university. Also, an athlete who did not participate in college football may be drafted four years after he entered college. Finally, the commissioner may grant eligibility through special permission. However, special permission has not been applied to allow a talented undergraduate to be drafted early.

The day after Red Grange played his last college game for Illinois in 1926 he signed a professional contract with the Chicago Bears *and* played in his first NFL game. Grange's actions led to an NFL rule that no athlete who practices or plays college football after the opening of the first NFL training camp may be under contract to, practice with, or play games for an NFL team during the balance of that season. Neither can a team directly or indirectly engage the services of a player until his college completes all games, including bowl games, in which the player is to participate.

Most legal observers of the draft believe that the NFL ban on drafting undergraduates would not stand up in court. However, any student-athlete who violates this NFL rule would also be violating an NCAA rule and would subject his team to possible forfeiture of games and loss of television revenue.

The NFL draft comprises 12 rounds by 28 teams, a total of 336 choices. If a player is not selected in the draft, he is a free agent and may sign with any team.

A player who is ineligible at the time of the draft but who becomes eligible before the start of the next NFL regular season may be selected in a supplemental draft. The team that picks him loses a comparable pick in the next regular draft. New Orleans, for example, lost its first-round pick in 1982 after selecting Illinois quarterback David Wilson in a supplemental draft. Wilson, who had transferred to Illinois, was declared ineligible for further college competition by the Big Ten Conference.

The NFL, which instituted its draft in 1936, holds its draft meeting in New York on the Tuesday and Wednesday on or before May 1 and 2. The collective bargaining agreement between the NFL Players Association and the league states that if a drafted player is not offered a contract by June 7 he is free to negotiate with any team. The agreement also sets out minimum contracts. The minimum amount varied in 1981 from $22,000 for a one-year contract to $40,000 for the first year of a series of four one-year contracts. (The typical procedure in the NFL is to offer two or more one-year contracts rather than one contract for several years.)

A player who receives at least the minimum contract offer by June 7 cannot negotiate with any other team (unless he is traded) until after the following year's draft. If selected again, he will still be limited to one team. If, however, he does not play professional football for two years, he is free to sign with any team.

Different rules apply to a player who is drafted by an NFL team but instead signs with a team in the Canadian Football League (CFL) or the United States Football League (USFL). In such cases, the original drafting team retains exclusive rights to the player for two years. After two years the player can negotiate with any NFL team, but the original team has the right to match any offer and sign the player. Tom Cousineau, for example, the Buffalo Bills' first-draft choice in the 1979 NFL draft, signed a two-year contract with Montreal of the Canadian Football League. As of March 1, 1982, he could negotiate with any NFL team, but the Buffalo Bills had the right to match any offer and sign their draft choice. When Houston offered Cousineau a reported $3.5 million contract for five years the Bills exercised their right to match and then traded Cousineau to the Cleveland Browns. Kansas City signed and retained cornerback Eric Harris in 1980 after he left Toronto of the CFL for a New Orleans offer.

The Canadian Football League also drafts college players. League rules restrict the number of U.S. citizens each team may employ. After failing to sign Herschel Walker in 1981, the CFL changed its draft rules to preclude the drafting of undergraduates.

The United States Football League (USFL), scheduled its first college draft for January 4, 1983. Prior to the draft each of the twelve teams would be able to claim 26 players from five colleges in the team's "territory." Each team could then draft 24 players in turn. Teams can trade territorial or regular draft rights.

The eligibility rules are the same as for the NFL. Since most college players who sign USFL contracts would have to leave school before the spring semester of their senior year to compete in the USFL's March-July season, the league offers a scholarship plan in its contracts. A one-year contract expires the following November 30, so that the player will remain the property of the USFL team through most of the following NFL season.

Basketball

The NBA draft takes place in June and continues for ten rounds. In 1981 the 23 teams drafted 230 players. Generally, a player becomes eligible for the draft the year his college eligibility expires. However, any player—including a high school senior—who has remaining eligibility (whether due to a transfer, an injury, or other reasons) may ask to be drafted by notifying the NBA, in writing at least 45 days before the draft, that he is renouncing his remaining collegiate eligibility.

In 1971, under court order resulting from the Spencer Haywood case, the NBA revised its rules to allow undergraduates to be drafted if they met a financial "hardship" test. This test is no longer required. The rule was virtually impossible to administer fairly and was the subject of legal action.

Although the NBA permits an athlete to withdraw from the draft up to 24 hours before the draft meeting, NCAA rules declare ineligible for a particular sport any athlete who has asked to be placed on a league's draft list. NBA teams may not contact an undergraduate until he has submitted his written request to be drafted. The commissioner may fine a team that violates this rule $250,000 and bar the team from ever drafting the player involved.

Each NBA team must offer contracts to its draft choices by September 5. The minimum contract offered must provide one of the following:

- One year at the minimum salary ($40,000 for 1981–82) with an option for a second year (at the club's discretion);
- Four years of $75,000, $90,000, $100,000, and $110,000, with $120,000 guaranteed;
- Five years of $75,000, $90,000, $100,000, and $110,000 and $125,000.

In practice, only lower-round draft choices are signed under the minimum terms. If the term complies with the minimum contract procedure and the player declines the offer, the team retains exclusive rights to the player until the next draft. The team also retains rights to a drafted player who opts to play in Europe, for one year after he reenters the NBA negotiating system.

Baseball

Baseball holds two drafts a year, in January and June. Most high school and four-year college players are drafted in June. The January draft pool consists primarily of junior college players. High school seniors or students whose eligibility has expired may be selected in June. Any draft choice who enters and remains in a four-year college without signing a contract may not be drafted again until he completes his junior year or turns 21 within 45 days of the June draft. If he is drafted at that point, the team has until the first day of classes in the fall to sign him. Otherwise, he becomes eligible for the June draft a year later. A junior college player may be drafted at any time and signed at any time except during his school's baseball season.

A four-year college student may make himself eligible for the draft by withdrawing from school or by transferring to a junior college. In either case, he must wait at least 120 days before he can sign a professional contract *and* he must be eligible to sign a contract within 45 days after the next draft. Otherwise, he cannot be drafted or signed until the second draft after he leaves the four-year college. For example, if a player withdraws from college on November 15 and the draft is held on January 20, he cannot be drafted until the June draft because the 120 days would not elapse until March 15, more than 45 days after the January draft.

Any team may talk with a high school or college player about his playing professional baseball even though he may not be eligible for the draft. No team may discuss contract terms other than asking the player what he expects for signing a contract.

After a team drafts a player, it must initiate negotiations within 15 days and offer a contract with a specific minor league team (or, in rare circumstances, with the major league team) at a salary in accordance with minimum and maximum figures set for each level of the minor leagues. These salary limits are:

- *Class AAA and AA:* $600 per month, except that it may be increased to $850 retroactive to the first day of active service with the AA or AAA club if the player is retained on the active service list for at least thirty days;
- *All other classifications*: at least $300, but not more than $700 per month.

The player cannot be offered a multiyear contract and must be guaranteed one month's salary.

Various rules govern bonuses. Although no limits apply to the amount of bonus paid for signing, bonus payments may not be deferred past the next calendar year after a player signs. A player may negotiate with a team to enter the College Scholarship Plan. This plan provides for payment of $1,000 a semester, up to $8,000 total, for college tuition, room, board, books, and fees as long as the player starts college within 18 months of signing the contract and does not miss two consecutive years without proper reason. In most instances, participation in winter league or instructional league play will extend college scholarship plan eligibility.

Since the baseball rules are complicated and contain numerous exceptions, any player with doubts about his status should write to the Office of the Commissioner, 15 West 51st Street, New York, NY 10019.

Hockey

The National Hockey League holds its draft annually in June. Any amateur (including Europeans) who will be 18 years old by September 15 of that year is eligible to be selected. If the drafting team offers a contract within one year, the player remains the property of that team until the next draft. If a drafted player enrolls in college rather than sign a contract, he remains the property of that team until he graduates or leaves school, plus 180 days. The team may trade the rights to that player. (For example, Rich Costello was traded by Philadelphia to Toronto during his freshman year at Providence College.) Unsigned players who do not enroll in college are again subject to the draft at age 19 or 20. After age 20 all undrafted amateurs (except Europeans) become free agents.

There is no minimum salary requirement for a minor league contract offered to a draft choice. The minimum for a contract to play in the NHL is $25,000, but the lowest paid player in 1981–82 received $55,000.

Soccer

The North American Soccer League (NASL) holds its primary draft each year in December. Teams may draft high school seniors, junior college players who have exhausted their junior college eligibility, and college players with no remaining soccer eligibility. In addition, any college player may ask the league to place him in the pool of players subject to the draft by submitting a letter not later than one week before the draft. The letter must be acknowledged by the athlete's coach or athletic director. By submitting the letter, an undergraduate forfeits all NCAA eligibility, regardless of whether or not he is drafted or signs an NASL contract. The NASL sends the NCAA a list of the undergraduates who petition to be drafted.

An NASL team retains its rights to college players until March 15. All college players unsigned at that point are eligible for the second-stage draft held in mid-March. Teams may not sign high school players until they have graduated. Any high school draft choice not signed by August 15 is eligible for the third-stage draft held in mid-August.

The Major Indoor Soccer League (MISL) holds its draft of amateur players after the end of the college soccer season. If a drafted player is not signed within one year, any team other than the one failing to sign him may draft him at the next draft. If no team selects him, he may sign with any team. But if a second team drafts him, it has one year to sign him or else he may sign with any team without restrictions. Finally, if a player plays in another soccer league before signing an MISL contract, the drafting team loses its rights to him.

B: Salary Information

Salary information for each sport is available to players from their players' association. Generally, the associations will provide an agent with access to the information upon the request of his client. Also, most players' associations will informally tell an agent how a contract offer to a client compares with terms obtained by other similarly situated players. However, the availability of information varies from sport to sport, depending in part on the association's access to the information and on the attitude of the association's staff toward cooperating with agents or particular agents.

Major Sports Salary Comparison

Sport	Year	Minimum	Average	Median
Baseball[a]	'81	32,000	186,651	135,000
	'82	33,500	250,000	
Basketball	'81-'82	40,000	215,000	165,000
Football	NFL '81	22,000 (rookie)	90,102	75,000
	CFL '81	18,000 ('82)	39,904[b]	
Hockey	'81-'82	25,000[c]	125,000	97,350

All figures from players' association unless otherwise noted.
Average and median figures rounded to thousands are estimates.

[a]Discounted 9 percent per year for salary deferrals without interest.
[b]Not including bonuses.
[c]Lowest actual salary was $55,000.

National Football League Salary Information, 1981

All salary figures in this report reflect a total of the following:
1. Base salary for 1981
2. Deferred compensation earned in 1981

Salary Information

3. Proportionate amount of signing bonus and/or compensation for negotiated option, pro-rated over number of contract years, including option year
4. Reporting bonus (for 1981 only)
5. Roster bonus (for making 1981 regular season roster)

Position	Players	Average	Median (midpoint)
Quarterbacks	85	$160,037	$128,750
Running Backs	196	94,948	75,000
Receivers	242	85,873	70,575
Offensive Linemen	290	85,543	77,500
Defensive Linemen	213	92,996	83,333
Linebackers	234	85,205	70,025
Defensive Backs	241	79,581	68,000
Kickers	61	65,779	63,167
	1,562	90,102	75,000

Major League Baseball Players Association
Average Salaries 1967–1982

Year	Minimum Salary	Average Salary	Median Salary
1967	$ 6,000	$ 19,000	$ 17,000
1968[a]	10,000	not available	not available
1969	10,000	24,909	19,750
1970	12,000	29,303	21,750
1971	12,750	31,543	24,750
1972	13,500	34,092	27,000
1973	15,000	36,566	28,000
1974	15,000	40,839	30,000
1975	16,000	44,676	34,000 estimate.
1976	19,000	51,501	40,000 "
1977	19,000	76,066	58,000 "
1978	21,000	99,876	68,000[b]
1979	21,000	113,558[c]	80,000[c]
1980	30,000	143,756[c]	95,000
1981	32,500	185,651[c]	135,000[c]
1982	33,500	250,000[d]	

[a]First Basic Agreement between Clubs and Major League Baseball Players Association.
[b]341 Players earned $68,000 or more; 342 players earned less than $68,000.
[c]Salary figures have been discounted for salary deferrals without interest at a rate of 9 percent per year for the period of delayed payments.
[d]Estimate.

Major League Baseball Players Association
Average Salaries by Position

Position	American League Number	American League 1981 Mean	National League Number	National League 1981 Mean	Both Leagues 1981 Mean	Both Leagues 1980 Mean	Both Leagues 1979 Mean
1st Base[a]	11	$324,933	9	$348,666	$335,613	$282,333	$222,397
2nd Base[a]	12	164,505	9	184,894	176,156	189,179	122,480
3rd Base[a]	12	229,953	12	259,651	244,802	202,833	163,257
Shortstop[a]	12	194,654	12	297,398	246,026	201,903	129,673
Catcher[a]	9	360,327	10	234,902	300,915	193,779	185,644
Outfielders[a]	38	280,421	30	323,907	299,666	232,163	178,934
Designated Hitter[b]	9	234,541	—	—	234,541	150,429	—
Pitcher[c]	62	195,690	50	235,901	213,608	173,400	139,126
Pitcher[d]	49	132,265	54	164,951	146,799	113,252	90,977

[a] 66 or more games
[b] 53 or more games
[c] 12 or more starts
[d] 7 or less starts, plus 17 relief appearances

Salary figures have been discounted for salary deferrals without interest, at a rate of 9 percent per year for the period of delayed payments.

National Basketball Association
Salary Information

Salaries for Individuals

Low	$ 40,000
Average	215,000
Median	165,000
High	2,200,000

These figures are based on NBA salary data for 1981–1982, except for the "high," which is the reported annual average value of the six-year contract Moses Malone signed with the Philadelphia '76ers in September 1982.

Team Average Salaries Per Player

Low	$160,000
Average	227,000
Median	251,000
High	390,000

The team average salaries have been calculated by adding the total fixed compensation for each player under contract as of January 1982 (including injured players) and dividing by the total length of the contracts (one to eight years, typically two to four).

National Hockey League Players' Association
Salary Survey, October–November, 1981

Category: 21 Clubs
Number Surveyed: 423

Salary Range $	Number	Percent of Total
Under 50,000	4	.9
51,000– 70,000	86	20.3
71,000– 90,000	98	23.2
91,000–110,000	74	17.5
111,000–130,000	62	14.7
131,000–150,000	34	8.0
151,000–170,000	14	3.3
171,000–190,000	18	4.3
191,000–210,000	11	2.6
211,000–250,000	7	1.7
Over 250,000	15	3.5
	423	100.0

Median: $97,350
Average Years Pro: 4.09
Average Age 25.07

C: Sample Contracts

The sample contracts that follow illustrate typical provisions in a player-agent agreement for negotiation of a playing contract, an athlete-investment manager agreement, and an athlete-financial manager agreement. They are not actual contracts, but were drafted by the Association of Representatives of Professional Athletes as a basis for a typical contract.

An athlete should be sure—*before* he signs any agreement—that the contract fits his own situation. The athlete should be especially wary of any contract that includes a power of attorney.

STANDARD PLAYER REPRESENTATIVE CONTRACT
[CONTRACT NEGOTIATION]

AGREEMENT made this _____ day of _____, 19 ____ by and between _____ (hereinafter called the "Representative") and _____ (hereinafter called the "Player") whose address is shown below.

WITNESSETH:

In consideration of the mutual promises hereinafter contained, the parties hereto agree as follows:

1. Term

The term of this Agreement shall begin on the date hereof and shall continue during the term of any player contract negotiated by the Representative on the Player's behalf pursuant to this Agreement and shall thereafter be deemed automatically renewed unless terminated as herein set forth. This Agreement may be terminated at any time by either party to be effective fifteen (15) days after notice of termination is given by either party to the other.

2. Contract Negotiation Services

The Representative shall represent, advise, counsel and assist the Player in the negotiation and execution of any and all player contracts for the performance of the Player's services as a professional athlete and the Representative shall continue to represent, advise, counsel and assist the Player in any and all dealings with the Player's professional athletic club relating to his player contract during the term of such player contract. The Representative acting in a fiduciary capacity shall be the Player's sole and exclusive representative in this regard, but shall not have the authority to bind or commit the Player in any way without the express prior consent of the Player.

3. Related Services

As part of the foregoing contract negotiation services to be rendered hereunder, and at no extra charge to the Player, the Representative shall provide to the Player other professional services, including, but not limited to, legal, accounting and estate planning services and such consultation regarding life and other forms of insurance as may be reasonably required in connection with the negotiation of all such player contracts.

4. Compensation

The Player shall pay to the Representative for services rendered hereunder a sum equal to the greater of either (i) the standard hourly rate charged by the Representative for such services up to a maximum of $ per hour or (ii)   percent (%) (not more than %) of all monies received by the Player as the gross amount of current and deferred salary (exclusive of playoff or post-season monies of any kind) under any player contract, including any substitutions, additions, modifications, renewals or extensions thereof, negotiated by the Representative on the Player's behalf during the term of this Agreement. Unless otherwise expressly agreed in writing by the parties hereto, the Player shall make all such fee payments to the Representative within fifteen (15) days of receipt of a salary payment under any aforesaid player contract or in such annual installments as may be agreed between the Player and the Representative. No such fee shall directly or indirectly be made payable or be paid to the Representative by the Player's professional athletic club or league, and the amount of such fee shall neither be agreed upon or discussed by the Representative with such professional athletic club or league.

5. Expenses

All expenses incurred by the Representative in the performance of the services hereunder shall be solely for the Representative's own account and shall not be reimbursable by the Player, except that the Player shall reimburse the Representative for travel and living expenses actually incurred by the Representative in an amount up to, but not to exceed without the express prior consent of the Player, One Thousand Dollars ($1,000.00) for negotiation of each separate player contract hereunder. The Player shall promptly pay all such expenses upon receipt of an itemized statement therefor.

6. Standards and Practices

In the performance of the services hereunder, the Representative shall abide by and conform to any and all uniform standards and practices published by the Joint Committee on Individual Representation established for such purpose by the major sports players associations.

7. Arbitration

The parties shall submit all disputes arising out of or relating to this Agreement to binding arbitration before the Impartial Arbitration panel created pursuant to the governing collective bargaining agreement in the sport in which the Player participates. Any such arbitration shall be held in accordance with the rules of the American Arbitration Association.

8. Notices

All notices hereunder shall be effective if sent by certified mail, postage prepaid, return receipt requested, as follows:

If to the Representative:

If to the Player:

9. Entire Agreement

This Agreement sets forth the entire agreement between the parties hereto and replaces or supersedes all prior agreements between the parties related to the same subject matter. This Agreement cannot be changed orally.

10. Governing Law

This Agreement shall be construed, interpreted and enforced according to the laws of the State of _____

**EXAMINE THIS CONTRACT CAREFULLY
BEFORE SIGNING IT**

IN WITNESS WHEREOF, the parties hereto have hereunder signed their names as hereinafter set forth.

PLAYER REPRESENTATIVE

PLAYER

NOTE: THIS FORM OF CONTRACT HAS BEEN APPROVED BY THE JOINT COMMITTEE ON INDIVIDUAL PLAYER REPRESENTATION ESTABLISHED BY THE MAJOR SPORTS PLAYERS ASSOCIATIONS. THIS CONTRACT SHOULD BE SIGNED AT LEAST IN TRIPLICATE. ONE COPY SHOULD BE PROMPTLY DELIVERED BY THE REPRESENTATIVE TO THE JOINT COMMITTEE ON INDIVIDUAL PLAYER REPRESENTATION, ONE COPY SHOULD BE PROMPTLY DELIVERED BY THE REPRESENTATIVE TO THE PLAYER AND ONE COPY SHOULD BE RETAINED BY THE REPRESENTATIVE.

STANDARD PLAYER INVESTMENT MANAGEMENT AGREEMENT

AGREEMENT and Power of Attorney made this _____ day of _____, 19_____ by and between _____ (hereinafter called the "Investment Manager") and _____ (hereinafter called the "Player") whose address is shown below.

WITNESSETH:

In consideration of the mutual promises hereinafter contained, the parties hereto agree as follows:

1. Term

The term of this Agreement and Power of Attorney shall be for a period of one (1) year beginning the date hereof and shall thereafter automatically continue on a year-to-year basis unless terminated as herein set forth. This Agreement and Power of Attorney may be terminated at any time by either party to be effective fifteen (15) days after notice of termination is given by either party to the other. In the event of termination, all cash, securities and other assets previously delivered by the Player to the Investment Manager as herein below set forth shall be returned to the Player on or before the effective date of termination.

2. Investment Services

Upon delivery to the Investment Manager by the Player of such cash, securities and other assets as the Player desires, the Investment Manager shall open an Investment Management Account to hold such cash, securities and other

Sample Contracts

assets together with any future stock dividends, rights or other distributions as agent in a fiduciary capacity pursuant to the Power of Attorney granted hereunder. Except as modified below under Special Instructions, the Investment Manager shall be authorized to utilize such discretion as is necessary to:

(a) hold, invest and reinvest the cash and securities at the Player's risk, at such times and in such manner as the Investment Manager shall determine;

(b) hold all or any part of such account uninvested for such period of time as the Investment Manager shall determine;

(c) vote in person or by proxy shares of stock or other securities in such manner as the Investment Manager shall determine;

(d) hold the property in the name of the Investment Manager's nominee; and

(e) sign the Player's name to any stock certificates, bonds or other securities registered in the Player's name in order to sell them or transfer them to the name of the Investment Manager's nominee.

3. **Special Instructions**

4. **Administrative Services**

The Investment Manager shall send the Player periodic statements on at least a quarterly basis showing principal and income transactions, and appraisals of the assets in the account and shall provide an annual statement of income collected, classified for federal income tax purposes, and a schedule of security transactions for the year showing gains and losses. For these purposes, the Player shall provide the Investment Manager with information as to the cost, date and manner of acquisition of the securities delivered to the Investment Manager by the Player or at his instruction and the Investment Manager may sign the Player's name to such certificates as may be required in connection with any tax laws. Unless otherwise set forth in the Special Instructions, the net amount of cash income received by the Investment Manager from the account is to be disposed of by accumulating and adding to the principal of the account on a monthly basis.

5. Compensation

The Investment Manager's compensation shall be based upon the market value of the Player's account when it opens and on subsequent anniversary dates, adjusted quarterly for interim additions and withdrawals of 10 percent or more, and will be at the following annual rates:

       % on the first $50,000
       % on the next $100,000
       % on the next $350,000
       % on the balance

The annual fee (minumum $) will be charged quarterly to the principal income in the Player's account.

6. Standards and Practices

In the performance of the services hereunder, the Investment Manager shall abide by and conform to any and all uniform standards and practices which from time to time may be recommended and published by the Joint Committee on Individual Player Representation established for such purpose by the major sports players associations.

7. Arbitration

The parties shall submit all disputes arising out of or relating to this Agreement and Power of Attorney to binding arbitration before the Impartial Arbitration panel created pursuant to the governing collective bargaining agreement in the sport in which the Player participates. Any such arbitration shall be held in accordance with the rules of the American Arbitration Association.

8. Notices

All notices hereunder shall be effective if sent by certified mail, postage prepaid, return receipt requested, as follows:

If to the Investment Manager:

If to the Player:

9. Entire Agreement

This Agreement and Power of Attorney sets forth the entire agreement between the parties hereto and replaces or supersedes all prior agreements between the parties related to the same subject matter. This Agreement and Power of Attorney cannot be changed orally.

10. Governing Law

This Agreement and Power of Attorney shall be construed, interpreted and enforced according to the laws of the State of _____

**EXAMINE THIS CONTRACT CAREFULLY
BEFORE SIGNING IT**

IN WITNESS WHEREOF, the parties hereto have hereunto signed their names as hereinafter set forth.

_____
INVESTMENT MANAGER

_____
PLAYER

NOTE: THIS FORM OF CONTRACT HAS BEEN APPROVED BY THE JOINT COMMITTEE ON INDIVIDUAL PLAYER REPRESENTATION ESTABLISHED BY THE MAJOR SPORTS PLAYERS ASSOCIATIONS. ONE COPY SHOULD BE PROMPTLY DELIVERED BY THE INVESTMENT MANAGER TO THE JOINT COMMITTEE ON INDIVIDUAL PLAYER REPRESENTATION, ONE COPY SHOULD BE PROMPTLY DELIVERED BY THE INVESTMENT MANAGER TO THE PLAYER AND ONE COPY SHOULD BE RETAINED BY THE INVESTMENT MANAGER.

STANDARD PLAYER PERSONAL FINANCIAL MANAGEMENT AGREEMENT

AGREEMENT and Power of Attorney made this _____ day of _____ 19_____ by and between _____ (hereinafter called the "Financial Manager") and _____ (hereinafter called the "Player") whose address is shown below.

WITNESSETH:

In consideration of the mutual promises hereinafter contained, the parties hereto agree as follows:

1. Term

The term of this Agreement and Power of Attorney shall be for a period of one (1) year beginning the date hereof and shall thereafter automatically continue on a year-to-year basis unless terminated as herein set forth. This Agreement and Power of Attorney may be terminated at any time by either party to be effective fifteen (15) days after notice of termination is given by either party to the other.

2. Financial Management Services

The Financial Manager acting in a fiduciary capacity shall represent, advise, counsel and assist the Player with respect to the personal financial affairs of the Player and shall maintain such affairs in an orderly and structured manner pursuant to the Power of Attorney granted hereunder. With respect thereto, the Financial Manager shall make available to the Player some or all of the following administrative services: (i) general bookkeeping services; (ii) programming with respect to the Player's budget, including the preparation of an annual financial summary; (iii) programming with respect to the Player's taxes and tax planning, including preparation of annual tax returns; (iv) payment of certain of the Player's expenses from funds supplied by the Player for that purpose; (v) periodic and detailed reports to the Player on the current status of his financial affairs; and (vi) such other advice and programming as may be deemed advisable by the Financial Manager in order to provide complete management of the Player's personal financial affairs as contemplated by this Agreement.

3. Related Services

In addition to the foregoing financial management services, and at no extra charge to the Player, the Financial Manager shall advise, counsel and assist the Player (i) in securing such other professional services, including, but not limited to, legal, accounting and estate planning services and such consultation regarding life and other forms of insurance as the Player may desire, or if qualified (ii) provide such services at the agreed upon regular hourly rate charged by the Financial Manager to other clients for similar services.

4. Compensation

The Player shall pay to the Financial Manager for services rendered hereunder a sum equal to   percent (%) (not more than   %) of the Player's annual gross income as adjusted in paragraph 5 below (or the allocable portion thereof exclusive of playoff or post-season monies of any kind) hereinafter earned by the Player for services rendered either as a professional athlete or in a non-professional capacity as a direct result of the Player's reputation as a professional athlete, including endorsements, individual licensing, promotions, personal appearances and the like. During the term of this Agreement and

Power of Attorney, the Financial Manager shall send to the Player at the end of each calendar quarter a statement for services rendered, and upon receipt thereof the Player shall promptly pay to the Financial Manager the quarterly charge for services rendered as set forth therein.

5. Expenses

All expenses incurred by the Financial Manager in the performances of the services hereunder shall be solely for the Financial Manager's own account and shall not be reimbursable by the Player, except that the Player shall pay or reimburse the Financial Manager for the fees and expenses of any attorney, accountant or other professional other than the Financial Manager engaged by or on behalf of the Player at the Player's request to render services to the Player. All fees and costs incurred by the Player for other professional services, whether rendered by the Financial Manager or such other professionals, shall be deducted from the annual gross income amount used in computing the percentage fee to which the Financial Manager is otherwise entitled hereunder. The Player shall promptly pay all such fees and costs upon receipt of an itemized statement therefor.

6. Standards and Practices

In the performance of the services hereunder, the Financial Manager shall abide by and conform to any and all uniform standards and practices which from time to time may be recommended and published by the Joint Committee on Individual Player Representation established for such purpose by the major sports players associations.

7. Arbitration

The parties shall submit all disputes arising out of or relating to this Agreement and Power of Attorney to binding arbitration before the Impartial Arbitration panel created pursuant to the governing collective bargaining agreement in the sport in which the Player participates. Any such arbitration shall be held in accordance with the rules of the American Arbitration Association.

8. Notices

All notices hereunder shall be effective if sent by certified mail, postage prepaid, return receipt requested, as follows:

If to the Financial Manager:

If to the Player:

9. Entire Agreement

This Agreement and Power of Attorney sets forth the entire agreement between the parties hereto and replaces or supersedes all prior agreements between the parties related to the same subject matter. This Agreement and Power of Attorney cannot be changed orally.

10. Governing Law

This Agreement and Power of Attorney shall be construed, interpreted and enforced according to the laws of the State of _____

**EXAMINE THIS CONTRACT CAREFULLY
BEFORE SIGNING IT**

IN WITNESS WHEREOF, the parties hereto have hereunto signed their names as hereinafter set forth.

_____
FINANCIAL MANAGER

_____
PLAYER

NOTE: THIS FORM OF CONTRACT HAS BEEN APPROVED BY THE JOINT COMMITTEE ON INDIVIDUAL PLAYER REPRESENTATION ESTABLISHED BY THE MAJOR SPORTS PLAYERS ASSOCIATIONS. THIS CONTRACT SHOULD BE SIGNED AT LEAST IN TRIPLICATE. ONE COPY SHOULD BE PROMPTLY DELIVERED BY THE FINANCIAL MANAGER TO THE JOINT COMMITTEE ON INDIVIDUAL PLAYER REPRESENTATION. ONE COPY SHOULD BE PROMPTLY DELIVERED BY THE FINANCIAL MANAGER TO THE PLAYER AND ONE COPY SHOULD BE RETAINED BY THE FINANCIAL MANAGER.

D: Uniform Players' Contracts

Each league has a standard contract which every player must sign. The contract form includes a blank line to insert the player's salary (Paragraph 2 in the baseball contract reprinted below and Paragraph 5 in the NFL contract below) and a blank space near the end to list special provisions such as bonuses.

Most of the terms of the contract are fixed as part of the collective bargaining agreement (basic agreement) between the league and the players' association. The agreement allows modifications in very few instances. One major exception concerns guaranteed contracts. For example, in the baseball contract Paragraph 7(b) of the Termination section can be modified to create a guaranteed contract. Copies of the standard contracts are available from the players' associations.

UNIFORM PLAYER'S CONTRACT
THE NATIONAL LEAGUE OF
PROFESSIONAL BASEBALL CLUBS

Parties

Between _____ herein called the Club,
and _____
of _____, herein called the Player.

Recital

The Club is a member of The National League of Professional Baseball Clubs, a voluntary association of member Clubs which has subscribed to the Major League Rules with The American League of Professional Baseball Clubs and its constituent Clubs and to The Professional Baseball Rules with that League and the National Association of Baseball Leagues.

Agreement

In consideration of the facts above recited and of the promises of each to the other, the parties agree as follows:

Employment

1. The Club hereby employs the Player to render, and the Player agrees to render, skilled services as a baseball player during the year(s) 19_____ including the Club's training season, the Club's exhibition games, the Club's playing season, the League Championship Series and the World Series (or any other official series in which the Club may participate and in any receipts of which the Player may be entitled to share).

Payment

2. For performance of the Player's services and promises hereunder the Club will pay the Player the sum of $_____

_____

in semi-monthly installments after the commencement of the playing season covered by this contract except as the schedule of payments may be modified by a special covenant. Payment shall be made on the day the amount becomes due, regardless of whether the Club is "home" or "abroad". If a monthly rate of payment is stipulated above, it shall begin with the commencement of the Club's playing season (or such subsequent date as the Player's services may commence) and end with the termination of the Club's scheduled playing season and shall be payable in semi-monthly installments as above provided.

Nothing herein shall interfere with the right of the Club and the Player by special covenant herein to mutually agree upon a method of payment whereby part of the Player's salary for the above year can be deferred to subsequent years.

If the Player is in the service of the Club for part of the playing season only, he shall receive such proportion of the sum above mentioned, as the number of days of his actual employment in the Club's playing season bears to the number of days in said season.

Notwithstanding the rate of payment stipulated above, the minimum rate of payment to the Player for each day of service on a Major League Club shall be at the rate of $30,000 per year for the 1980 playing season, $32,500 per year for the 1981 playing season, $33,500 per year for the 1982 playing season, and $35,000 per year for the 1983 playing season. Effective with the 1981 championship season, the minimum rate of payment for National Association service for all Players (a) signing a second Major League contract (not convering the same season as any such Player's initial Major League contract) or a subsequent Major League contract, or (b) having at least one day of Major League Service, shall be at the rate of $14,000 per year for the 1981 and 1982 playing seasons, and $16,000 per year for the 1983 playing season.

Payment to the Player at the rate stipulated above shall be continued throughout any period in which a Player is required to attend a regularly scheduled military encampment of the Reserve of the Armed Forces or of the National Guard during the Club's playing season.

Loyalty

3.(a) The Player agrees to perform his services hereunder diligently and faithfully, to keep himself in first-class physical condition and to obey the Club's training rules, and pledges himself to the American public and to the Club to conform to high standards of personal conduct, fair play and good sportsmanship.

Baseball Promotion

3.(b) In addition to his services in connection with the actual playing of baseball, the Player agrees to cooperate with the Club and participate in any and all reasonable promotional activities of the Club and its League, which, in the opinion of the Club, will promote the welfare of the Club or professional baseball, and to observe and comply with all reasonable requirements of the Club respecting conduct and service of its team and its players, at all times whether on or off the field.

Pictures and Public Appearances

3.(c) The Player agrees that his picture may be taken for still photographs, motion pictures or television at such times as the Club may designate and agrees that all rights in such pictures shall belong to the Club and may be used by the Club for publicity purposes in any manner it desires. The Player further agrees that during the playing season he will not make public appearances, participate in radio or television programs or permit his picture to be taken or write or sponsor newspaper or magazine articles or sponsor commercial products without the written consent of the Club, which shall not be withheld except in the reasonable interests of the Club or professional baseball.

PLAYER REPRESENTATIONS
Ability

4.(a) The Player represents and agrees that he has exceptional and unique skill and ability as a baseball player; that his services to be rendered hereunder are of a special, unusual and extraordinary character which gives them peculiar value which cannot be reasonably or adequately compensated for in damages at law, and that the Player's breach of this contract will cause the Club great and irreparable injury and damage. The Player agrees that, in addition to other remedies, the Club shall be entitled to injunctive and other equitable relief to prevent a breach of his contract by the Player, including, among others, the right to enjoin the Player from playing baseball for any other person or organization during the term of his contract.

Condition

4.(b) The Player represents that he has no physical or mental defects known to him and unknown to the appropriate representative of the Club which would prevent or impair performance of his services.

Interest in Club

4.(c) The player represents that he does not, directly or indirectly, own stock or have any financial interest in the ownership or earnings of any Major League Club, except as hereinafter expressly set forth, and covenants that he will not hereafter, while connected with any Major League Club, acquire or hold any such stock or interest except in accordance with Major League Rule 20(e).

Service

5.(a) The Player agrees that, while under contract, and prior to expiration of the Club's right to renew this contract, he will not play baseball otherwise than for the Club, except that the Player may participate in post-season games under the conditions prescribed in the Major League Rules. Major League Rule 18(b) is set forth herein.

Other Sports

5.(b) The Player and the Club recognize and agree that the Player's participation in certain other sports may impair or destroy his ability and skill as a baseball player. Accordingly, the Player agrees that he will not engage in professional boxing or wrestling; and that, except with the written consent of the Club, he will not engage in skiing, auto racing, motorcycle racing, sky diving, or in any game or exhibition of football, soccer, professional league basketball, ice hockey or other sport involving a substantial risk of personal injury.

Assignment

6.(a) The Player agrees that this contract may be assigned by the Club (and reassigned by any assignee Club) to any other Club in accordance with the Major League Rules and Professional Baseball Rules. The Club and the Player may, without obtaining special approval, agree by special covenant to limit or eliminate the right of the Club to assign this contract.

Medical Information

6.(b) The Player agrees that, should the Club contemplate an assignment of this contract to another Club or Clubs, the Club's physician may furnish to the physicians and officials of such other Club or Clubs all relevant medical information relating to the Player.

Uniform Players' Contracts

No Salary Reduction

6.(c) The amount stated in paragraph 2 and in special covenants hereof which is payable to the Player for the period stated in paragraph 1 hereof shall not be diminished by any such assignment, except for failure to report as provided in the next subparagraph (d).

Reporting

6.(d) The Player shall report to the assignee Club promptly (as provided in the Regulation) upon receipt of written notice from the Club of the assignment of this contract. If the Player fails to so report, he shall not be entitled to any payment for the period from the date he receives written notice of assignment until he reports to the assignee Club.

Obligations of Assignor and Assignee Clubs

6.(e) Upon and after such assignment, all rights and obligations of the assignor Club hereunder shall become the rights and obligations of the assignee Club; provided, however, that

(1) The assignee Club shall be liable to the Player for payments accruing only from the date of assignment and shall not be liable (but the assignor Club shall remain liable) for payments accrued prior to that date.

(2) If at any time the assignee is a Major League Club, it shall be liable to pay the Player at the full rate stipulated in paragraph 2 hereof for the remainder of the period stated in paragraph 1 hereof and all prior assignors and assignees shall be relieved of liability for any payment for such period.

(3) Unless the assignor and assignee Clubs agree otherwise, if the assignee Club is a National Association Club, the assignee Club shall be liable only to pay the Player at the rate usually paid by said assignee Club to other Players of similar skill and ability in its classification and the assignor Club shall be liable to pay the difference for the remainder of the period stated in paragraph 1 hereof between an amount computed at the rate stipulated in paragraph 2 hereof and the amount so payable by the assignee Club.

Moving Allowances

6.(f) The Player shall be entitled to moving allowances under the circumstances and in the amounts set forth in Article VII of the Basic Agreement between the Major League Clubs and the Major League Baseball Players Association, effective January 1, 1980.

"Club"

6.(g) All references in other paragraphs of this contract to "the Club" shall be deemed to mean and include any assignee of this contract.

TERMINATION

By Player

7.(a) The Player may terminate this contract, upon written notice to the Club, if the Club shall default in the payments to the Player provided for in paragraph 2 hereof or shall fail to perform any other obligation agreed to be performed by the Club hereunder and if the Club shall fail to remedy such default within ten (10) days after the receipt by the Club of written notice of such default. The Player may also terminate this contract as provided in subparagraph (d)(4) of this paragraph 7. (See Article XIV H of Basic Agreement effective January 1, 1980.)

By Club

7.(b) The Club may terminate this contract upon written notice to the Player (but only after requesting and obtaining waivers of this contract from all other Major League Clubs) if the Player shall at any time:

(1) fail, refuse or neglect to conform his personal conduct to the standards of good citizenship and good sportsmanship or to keep himself in first-class physical condition or to obey the Club's training rules; or

(2) fail, in the opinion of the Club's management, to exhibit sufficient skill or competitve ability to qualify or continue as a member of the Club's team; or

(3) fail, refuse or neglect to render his services hereunder or in any other manner materially breach this contract.

7.(c) If this contract is terminated by the Club, the Player shall be entitled to termination pay under the circumstances and in the amounts set forth in Article VIII of the Basic Agreement between the Major League Clubs and the Major League Baseball Players Association, effective January 1, 1980. In addition, the Player shall be entitled to receive an amount equal to the reasonable traveling expenses of the Player, including first-class jet air fare and meals en route, to his home city.

Procedure

7.(d) If the Club proposes to terminate this contract in accordance with subparagraph (b) of this paragraph 7, the procedure shall be as follows:

(1) The Club shall request waivers from all other Major League Clubs. Such waivers shall be good for six (6) days only. Such waiver request must state that it is for the purpose of terminating this contract and it may not be withdrawn.

(2) Upon receipt of waiver request, any other Major League Club may claim assignment of this contract at a waiver price of $1.00, the priority of claims to be determined in accordance with the Major League Rules.

(3) If this contract is so claimed, the Club shall, promptly and before any assignment, notify the Player that it had requested waivers for the purpose of terminating this contract and that the contract had been claimed.

(4) Within 5 days after receipt of notice of such claim, the Player shall be entitled, by written notice to the Club, to terminate this contract on the date of his notice of termination. If the Player fails to so notify the Club, this contract shall be assigned to the claiming Club.

(5) If the contract is not claimed, the Club shall promptly deliver written notice of termination to the Player at the expiration of the waiver period.

7.(e) Upon any termination of this contract by the Player, all obligations of both Parties hereunder shall cease on the date of termination, except the obligation of the Club to pay the Player's compensation to said date.

Regulations

8. The Player accepts as part of this contract the Regulations set forth herein.

Rules

9.(a) The Club and the Player agree to accept, abide by and comply with all provisions of the Major League Agreement, the Major League Rules, the Rules or Regulations of the League of which the Club is a member, and the Professional Baseball Rules, in effect on the date of this Uniform Player's Contract, which are not inconsistent with the provisions of this contract or the provisions of any agreement between the Major League Clubs and the Major League Baseball Players Association, provided that the Club, together with the other clubs of the American and National Leagues and the National Association, reserves the right to modify, supplement or repeal any provision of said Agreement, Rules and/or Regulations in a manner not inconsistent with this contract or the provisions of any then existing agreement between the Major League Clubs and the Major League Baseball Players Association.

Disputes

9.(b) All disputes between the Player and the Club which are covered by the Grievance Procedure as set forth in the Basic Agreement, effective January 1, 1980, shall be resolved in accordance with such Grievance Procedure.

Publication

9.(c) The Club, the League President and the Commissioner, or any of them, may make public the findings, decision and record of any inquiry, investigation or hearing held or conducted, including in such record all evidence or information, given, received, or obtained in connection therewith.

Renewal

10.(a) Unless the Player has exercised his right to become a free agent as set forth in the Basic Agreement between the Major League Clubs and the Major League Baseball Players Association, effective January 1, 1980, the Club may, on or before December 20 (or if a Sunday, then the next preceding business day) in the year of the last playing season covered by this contract, tender to the

Player a contract for the term of the next year by mailing the same to the Player at his address following his signature hereto, or if none be given, then at his last address of record with the Club. If prior to the March 1 next succeeding said December 20, the Player and the Club have not agreed upon the terms of such contract, then on or before 10 days after said March 1, the Club shall have the right by written notice to the Player at said address to renew this contract for the period of one year on the same terms, except that the amount payable to the Player shall be such as the Club shall fix in said notice; provided, however, that said amount, if fixed by a Major League Club, shall be an amount payable at a rate not less than as specified in Article V, Section C, of the Basic Agreement. Subject to the Player's rights as set forth in the Basic Agreement, effective January 1, 1980, the Club may renew this contract from year to year.

10.(b) The Club's right to renew this contract, as provided in subparagraph (a) of this paragraph 10, and the promise of the Player not to play otherwise than with the Club have been taken into consideration in determining the amount payable under paragraph 2 hereof.

Governmental Regulation—National Emergency

11. This contract is subject to federal or state legislation, regulations, executive or other official orders or other governmental action, now or hereafter in effect respecting military, naval, air or other governmental service, which may directly or indirectly affect the Player, Club or the League and subject also to the right of the Commissioner to suspend the operation of this contract during any national emergency during which Major League Baseball is not played.

Commissioner

12. The term "Commissioner" wherever used in this contract shall be deemed to mean the Commissioner designated under the Major League Agreement, or in the case of a vacancy in the office of Commissioner, the Executive Council or such other body or person or persons as shall be designated in the Major League Agreement to exercise the powers and duties of the Commissioner during such vacancy.

Supplemental Agreements

The Club and the Player covenant that this contract, the Basic Agreement effective January 1, 1980 and the Agreement Re Major League Baseball Players Benefit Plan effective April 1, 1980 fully set forth all understandings and agreements between them, and agree that no other understandings or agreements, whether heretofore or hereafter made, shall be valid, recognizable, or of any effect whatsoever, unless expressly set forth in a new or supplemental contract executed by the Player and the Club (acting by its President or such other officer as shall have been thereunto duly authorized by the President or Board of Directors as evidenced by a certificate filed of record with the League President and Commissioner) and complying with the Major League Rules and the Professional Baseball Rules.

REGULATIONS

1. The Club's playing season for each year covered by this contract and all renewals hereof shall be as fixed by The National League of Professional Baseball Clubs, or if this contract shall be assigned to a Club in another League, then by the League of which such assignee is a member.

2. The Player, when requested by the Club, must submit to a complete physical examination at the expense of the Club, and if necessary to treatment by a regular physician or dentist in good standing. Upon refusal of the Player to submit to a complete medical or dental examination the Club may consider such refusal a violation of this regulation and may take such action as it deems advisable under Regulation 5 of this contract. Disability directly resulting from injury sustained in the course and within the scope of his employment under this contract shall not impair the right of the Player to receive his full salary for the period of such disability or for the the season in which the injury was sustained (whichever period is shorter), together with the reasonable medical and hospital expenses incurred by reason of the injury and during the term of this contract or for a period of up to two years from the date of initial treatment for such injury, whichever period is longer, but only upon the express prerequisite conditions that (a) written notice of such injury, including the time, place, cause and nature of the injury, is served upon and received by the Club within twenty days of the sustaining of said injury and (b) the Club shall have the right to designate the doctors and hospitals furnishing such medical and hospital services. Failure to give such notice shall not impair the rights of the Player, as herein set forth, if the Club has actual knowledge of such injury. All workmen's compensation payments received by the Player as compensation for loss of income for a specific period during which the Club is paying him in full, shall be paid over by the Player to the Club. Any other disability may be ground for suspending or terminating this contract.

3. The Club will furnish the Player with two complete uniforms, exclusive of shoes, unless the Club requires the Player to wear non-standard shoes in which case the Club will furnish the shoes. The uniforms will be surrendered by the Player to the Club at the end of the season or upon termination of this contract.

4. The Player shall be entitled to expense allowances under the circumstances and in the amounts set forth in Article VI of the Basic Agreement between the Major League Clubs and the Major League Baseball Players Association, effective January 1, 1980.

5. For violation by the Player of any regulation or other provision of this contract, the Club may impose a reasonable fine and deduct the amount thereof from the Player's salary or may suspend the Player without salary for a period not exceeding thirty days or both. Written notice of the fine or suspension or both and the reason therefor shall in every case be given to the Player and the Players Association. (See Article XI of Basic Agreement effective January 1, 1980.)

6. In order to enable the Player to fit himself for his duties under this contract, the Club may require the Player to report for practice at such places as the Club may designate and to participate in such exhibition contests as may be arranged by the Club, without any other compensation than that herein elsewhere provided, for a period beginning not earlier than March 1 or ten days prior to the second Saturday in March, whichever is earlier, provided, however, that the Club may invite pitchers and catchers to report at an earlier date on a voluntary basis. The Club will pay the necessary traveling expenses, including the first-class jet air fare and meals en route of the Player from his home city to the training place of the Club, whether he be ordered to go there directly or by way of the home city of the Club. In the event of the failure of the Player to report for practice or to participate in the exhibition games, as required and provided for, he shall be required to get into playing condition to the satisfaction of the Club's team manager, and at the Player's own expense, before his salary shall commence.

7. In case of assignment of this contract the Player shall report promptly to the assignee Club within 72 hours from the date he receives written notice from the Club of such assignment, if the Player is then not more than 1,600 miles by most direct available railroad route from the assignee Club, plus an additional 24 hours for each additional 800 miles.

Post-Season Exhibition Games. Major League Rule 18(b) provides:

(b) EXHIBITION GAMES. No player shall participate in any exhibition game during the period between the close of the Major League championship season and the following training season, except that, with the consent of his club and permission of the Commissioner, a player may participate in exhibition games for a period of not less than thirty (30) days, such period to be designated annually by the Commissioner. Players who participate in barnstorming during this period cannot engage in any Winter League activities. Player conduct, on and off the field, in connection with such post-season exhibition games shall be subject to the discipline of the Commissioner. The Commissioner shall not approve of more than three (3) players of any one club on the same team. The Commissioner shall not approve of more than three (3) players from the joint membership of the World Series participants playing in the same game. No player shall participate in any exhibition game with or against any team which, during the current season or within one year, has had any ineligible player or which is or has been during the current season or within one (1) year, managed and controlled by an ineligible player or by any person who has listed an ineligible player under an assumed name or who otherwise has violated, or attempted to violate, any exhibition game contract; or with or against any team which, during said season or within one (1) year, has played against teams containing such ineligible players, or so managed or controlled. Any player violating this Rule shall be fined not less than Fifty Dollars ($50.00) nor more than Five Hundred Dollars ($500.00), except that in no event shall such fine be less than the consideration received by such player for participating in such game.

Special Covenants

Approval

This contract or any supplement hereto shall not be valid or effective unless and until approved by the League President.

Signed in duplicate this _____ day of _____, A.D. 198__

_____
(Player)

_____
(Home address of Player)

Social Security No. _____

Approved _____, 198__

_____
President, The National League of Professional Baseball Clubs

_____
(Club)

By _____
(Authorized Signature)

NFL PLAYER CONTRACT

THIS CONTRACT is between _____, hereinafter "Player," and _____, a _____corporation (limited partnership) (partnership), hereinafter "Club," operating under the name of the _____

as a member of the National Football League, hereinafter "League." In consideration of the promises made by each to the other, Player and Club agree as follows:

1. TERM. This contract covers one football season, and will begin on the date of execution or April 1, 19 ____, whichever is later, and end on April 1, 19 ____, unless extended, terminated, or renewed as specified elsewhere in this contract.

2. EMPLOYMENT AND SERVICES. Club employs Player as a skilled football player. Player accepts such employment. He agrees to give his best efforts and loyalty to the Club, and to conduct himself on and off the field with appropriate recognition of the fact that the success of professional football depends largely on public respect for and approval of those associated with the game. Player will report promptly for and participate fully in Club's official pre-season training camp, all Club meetings and practice sessions, and all pre-season, regular-season and post-season football games scheduled for or by Club. If invited, Player will practice for and play in any all-star football game sponsored by the League. Player will not participate in any football game not sponsored by the League unless the game is first approved by the League.

3. OTHER ACTIVITIES. Without prior written consent of Club, Player will not play football or engage in activities related to football otherwise than for Club or engage in any activity other than football which may involve a significant risk of personal injury. Player represents that he has special, exceptional and unique knowledge, skill, ability, and experience as a football player, the loss of which cannot be estimated with any certainty and cannot be fairly or adequately compensated by damages. Player therefore agrees that Club will have the right, in addition to any other right which Club may possess, to enjoin Player by appropriate proceedings from playing football or engaging in football-related activities other than for Club or from engaging in any activity other than football which may involve a significant risk of personal injury.

4. PUBLICITY. Player grants to Club and League, separately and together, the authority to use his name and picture for publicity and promotional purposes in newspapers, magazines, motion pictures, game programs and roster manuals, broadcasts and telecasts, and all other publicity and advertising media, provided such publicity and promotion does not in itself constitute an endorsement by Player of a commercial product. Player will cooperate with the news media, and will participate upon request in reasonable promotional activities of Club and the League.

5. COMPENSATION. For performance of Player's services and all other promises of Player, Club will pay Player a yearly salary of $_____, payable as provided in Paragraph 6; such earned performance bonuses as may be called for in Paragraph 24 of or any attachment to this contract; Player's necessary traveling expenses from his residence to training camp; Player's reasonable board and lodging expenses during pre-season training and in connection with playing pre-season, regular-season, and post-season football games outside

Club's home city; Player's necessary traveling expenses to and from pre-season, regular-season, and post-season football games outside Club's home city; Player's necessary traveling expenses to his residence if this contract is terminated by Club; and such additional compensation, benefits and reimbursement of expenses as may be called for in any collective bargaining agreement in existence during the term of this contract. (For purposes of this contract, a collective bargaining agreement will be deemed to be "in existence" during its stated term or during any period for which the parties to that agreement agree to extend it.)

6. PAYMENT. Unless this contract or any collective bargaining agreement in existence during the term of this contract specifically provides otherwise, Player will be paid as follows: If Player has not previously reported to any NFL club's official pre-season training camp in any year, he will be paid 100% of his yearly salary under this contract in equal weekly or bi-weekly installments over the course of the regular season period, commencing with the first regular season game played by club. If Player has previously reported to any NFL club's official pre-season training camp in any year, he will be paid 10% of his yearly salary under this contract in equal weekly installments over the course of the pre-season period, commencing with the end of the first week of Club's official pre-season training camp as designated for Player and ending one week prior to the first regular season game played by Club, and 90% of his yearly salary in equal weekly or bi-weekly installments over the course of the regular season period, commencing with the first regular season game played by Club. If this contract is executed or Player is activated after the start of Club's official pre-season training camp, the yearly salary payable to Player will be reduced proportionately and Player will be paid the weekly or bi-weekly portions of his yearly salary becoming due and payable after he is activated. If this contract is terminated after the start of Club's official pre-season training camp, the yearly salary payable to Player will be reduced proportionately and Player will be paid the weekly or bi-weekly portions of his yearly salary having become due and payable up to the time of termination (prorated daily if termination occurs before one week prior to the first regular season game played by Club).

7. DEDUCTIONS. Any advance made to Player will be repaid to Club, and any properly levied Club fine or Commissioner fine against Player will be paid, in cash on demand or by means of deductions from payments coming due to the Player under this contract, the amount of such deductions to be determined by Club unless this contract specifically provides otherwise.

8. PHYSICAL CONDITION. Player represents to Club that he is and will maintain himself in excellent physical condition. Player will undergo a complete physical examination by the Club physician upon Club request, during which physical examination Player agrees to make full and complete disclosure of any physical or mental condition known to him which might impair his perfor-

mance under this contract and to respond fully and in good faith when questioned by the Club physician about such condition. If Player fails to establish or maintain his excellent physical condition to the satisfaction of the Club physician, or make the required full and complete disclosure and good faith responses to the Club physician, then Club may terminate this contract.

9. INJURY. If Player is injured in the performance of his services under this contract and promptly reports such injury to the Club physician or trainer, then Player will receive such medical and hospital care during the term of this contract as the Club physician may deem necessary, and, in accordance with Club's practice, will continue to receive his yearly salary for so long, during the season of injury only and for no subsequent period, as Player is physically unable to perform the services required of him by this contract because of such injury. If Player's injury in the performance of his services under this contract results in his death, the unpaid balance of his yearly salary for the season of injury will be paid to his stated beneficiary or, in the absence of a stated beneficiary, to his estate.

10. WORKMEN'S COMPENSATION. Any compensation paid to Player under this contract or under any collective bargaining agreement in existence during the term of this contract for a period during which he is entitled to workmen's compensation benefits by reason of temporary total, permanent total, temporary partial, or permanent partial disability will be deemed an advance payment of workmen's compensation benefits due Player, and Club will be entitled to be reimbursed the amount of such payment out of any award of workmen's compensation.

11. SKILL, PERFORMANCE AND CONDUCT. Player understands that he is competing with other players for a position on Club's roster within the applicable player limits. If at any time, in the sole judgment of Club, Player's skill or performance has been unsatisfactory as compared with that of other players competing for positions on Club's roster, or if Player has engaged in personal conduct reasonably judged by Club to adversely affect or reflect on Club, then Club may terminate this contract.

12. TERMINATION. The rights of termination set forth in this contract will be in addition to any other rights of termination allowed either party by law. Termination will be effective upon the giving of written notice, except that Player's death, other than as a result of injury incurred in the performance of his services under this contract, will automatically terminate this contract. If this contract is terminated by Club and either Player or Club so requests, Player will promptly undergo a complete physical examination by the Club physician.

13. INJURY GRIEVANCE. Unless a collective bargaining agreement in existence at the time of termination of this contract by Club provides otherwise, the following injury grievance procedure will apply: If Player believes that at

the time of termination of this contract by Club he was physically unable to perform the services required of him by this contract because of an injury incurred in the performance of his services under this contract, Player may, within a reasonably brief time after examination by the Club physician, submit at his own expense to examination by a physician of his choice. If the opinion of Player's physician with respect to his physical ability to perform the services required of him by this contract is contrary to that of the Club's physician, the dispute will be submitted within a reasonable time to final and binding arbitration by an arbitrator selected by Club and Player or, if they are unable to agree, one selected by the League Commissioner on application by either party.

14. RULES. Player will comply with and be bound by all reasonable Club rules and regulations in effect during the term of this contract which are not inconsistent with the provisions of this contract or of any collective bargaining agreement in existence during the term of this contract. Player's attention is also called to the fact that the League functions with certain rules and procedures expressive of its operation as a joint venture among its member clubs and that these rules and practices may affect Player's relationship to the League and its member clubs independently of the provisions of this contract.

15. INTEGRITY OF GAME. Player recognizes the detriment to the League and professional football that would result from impairment of public confidence in the honest and orderly conduct of NFL games or the integrity and good character of NFL players. Player therefore acknowledges his awareness that if he accepts a bribe or agrees to throw or fix an NFL game; fails to promptly report a bribe offer or an attempt to throw or fix an NFL game; bets on an NFL game; knowingly associates with gamblers or gambling activity; uses or provides other players with stimulants or other drugs for the purpose of attempting to enhance on-field performance; or is guilty of any other form of conduct reasonably judged by the League Commissioner to be detrimental to the League or professional football, the Commissioner will have the right, but only after giving Player the opportunity for a hearing at which he may be represented by counsel of his choice, to fine Player in a reasonable amount; to suspend Player for a period certain or indefinitely; and/or to terminate this contract.

16. EXTENSION. If Player becomes a member of the Armed Forces of the United States or any other country, or retires from professional football as an active player, or otherwise fails or refuses to perform his services under this contract, then this contract will be tolled between the date of Player's induction into the Armed Forces, or his retirement, or his failure or refusal to perform, and the later date of his return to professional football. During the period this contract is tolled, Player will not be entitled to any compensation or benefits. On Player's return to professional football, the term of this contract will be extended for a period of time equal to the number of seasons (to the nearest multiple of one) remaining at the time the contract was tolled. The right of

renewal, if any, contained in this contract will remain in effect until the end of any such extended term.

17. RENEWAL. Unless this contract specifically provides otherwise, Club may, by sending written notice to Player on or before the April 1 expiration date referred to in Paragraph 1, renew this contract for a period of one year. The terms and conditions for the renewal year will be the same as those provided in this contract for the last preceding year, except that there will be no further right of renewal in Club and, unless this contract specifically provides otherwise, the rate of compensation for the renewal year will be 90% of the rate of compensation provided in this contract for the last preceding year. The phrase "rate of compensation" as used above means yearly salary, including deferred compensation, and any performance bonus, but excluding any signing or reporting bonus. In order for Player to receive 90% of any performance bonus under this contract he must meet the previously established conditions of that bonus during the renewal year.

18. ASSIGNMENT. Unless this contract specifically provides otherwise, Club may assign this contract and Player's services under this contract to any successor to Club's franchise or to any other Club in the League. Player will report to the assignee club promptly upon being informed of the assignment of his contract and will faithfully perform his services under this contract. The assignee club will pay Player's necessary traveling expenses in reporting to it and will faithfully perform this contract with Player.

19. FILING. This contract will be valid and binding upon Player and Club immediately upon execution. A copy of this contract, including any attachment to it, will be filed by Club with the League Commissioner within 10 days after execution. The Commissioner will have the right to disapprove this contract on reasonable grounds, including but not limited to an attempt by the parties to abridge or impair the rights of any other club, uncertainty or incompleteness in expression of the parties' respective rights and obligations, or conflict between the terms of this contract and any collective bargaining agreement then in existence. Approval will be automatic unless, within 10 days after receipt of this contract in his office, the Commissioner notifies the parties either of disapproval or of extension of this 10-day period for purposes of investigation or clarification pending his decision. On the receipt of notice of disapproval and termination, both parties will be relieved of their respective rights and obligations under this contract.

20. DISPUTES. Any dispute between Player and Club involving the interpretation or application of any provision of this contract will be submitted to final and binding arbitration in accordance with the procedure called for in any collective bargaining agreement in existence at the time the event giving rise to any such dispute occurs. If no collective bargaining agreement is in existence at such time, the dispute will be submitted within a reasonable time to the League

Commissioner for final and binding arbitration by him, except as provided otherwise in Paragraph 13 of this contract.

21. NOTICE. Any notice, request, approval or consent under this contract will be sufficiently given if in writing and delivered in person or mailed (certified or first class) by one party to the other at the address set forth in this contract or to such other address as the recipient may subsequently have furnished in writing to the sender.

22. OTHER AGREEMENTS. This contract, including any attachment to it, sets forth the entire agreement between Player and Club and cannot be modified or supplemented orally. Player and Club represent that no other agreement, oral or written, except as attached to or specifically incorporated in this contract, exists between them. The provisions of this contract will govern the relationship between Player and Club unless there are conflicting provisions in any collective bargaining agreement in existence during the term of this contract, in which case the provisions of the collective bargaining agreement will take precedence over conflicting provisions of this contract relating to the rights or obligations of either party.

23. LAW. This contract is made under and shall be governed by the laws of the State of _____

24. SPECIAL PROVISIONS.

THIS CONTRACT is executed in triplicate this _____ day of _____, 19_____. Player acknowledges that before signing this contract he was given the opportunity to seek advice from or be represented by persons of his own selection.

PLAYER

Home Address

Telephone Number

CLUB

By

Club Address

League Office Copy

E: Agent Authorization Form

Baseball is the only sport which requires that its teams deal only with agents authorized in writing by a player to represent that player. The player must file an authorization form with his team when he retains an agent for the first time, changes agents, or signs a new playing contract. Any team which deals with an unauthorized agent may be disciplined by the Commissioner.

The purpose of this requirement is to reduce the risk that anyone will pose as an agent for a player who has not retained him. The registration list also enables the Commissioner and the Players Association to inform agents about matters such as the complex rules concerning the free agent process.

A copy of the Commissioner's notice about the authorization requirement and a copy of the authorization form follow.

OFFICE OF THE COMMISSIONER
15 West 51st Street, In Rockefeller Center
New York, N. Y. 10019
Telephone (212) 586-7400

NOTICE NO. 27   August 20, 1981

TO: ALL MAJOR LEAGUE CLUBS
      ALL MAJOR LEAGUE PLAYERS
      ALL MAJOR LEAGUE PLAYER AGENTS

RE: MAJOR LEAGUE RULE 3(g)—TAMPERING

Gentlemen:

It is once again appropriate for me to remind all concerned of their responsibilities and obligations under Major League Rule 3(g), which defines tampering. While there are changes in the new amendments to the Basic Agreement relating to the Re-Entry Draft, the Basic Agreement does not affect the applicability of the tampering rule to players under contract or reservation. This most important rule therefore remains in full force and effect now and throughout the year.

Major League Rule 3(g) provides in part as follows:

"(g) TAMPERING. To preserve discipline and competition, and to prevent the enticement of players. . . , there shall be no negotiations or dealings respecting employment, either present or perspective, between any player . . . and any Club other than the Club with which he is under contract or acceptance of terms, or by which he is reserved . . . unless the Club . . . with which he is connected shall have, in writing, expressly authorized such negotiations or dealings prior to their commencement."

Accordingly, all recipients of this bulletin are requested to bear the following in mind:

1) *Persons Affected*: The no-tampering rule is binding on Clubs and players alike.

a) *Clubs*: The rule is binding on all Club personnel, including owners, officers, directors, officials, administrative staff, scouts, field manager, coaches, trainer, team physician, etc. *Clubs are therefore asked to circulate this bulletin throughout their organizations.*

b) *Players*: So long as players are under contract or reservation to a Club, they are subject to the Rule. The fact that a player may be in a position to qualify for the Re-Entry Draft at the end of the season does not change the binding nature of the Rule as to him.

2) *Conduct Prohibited*: As the terms of Rule 3(g) make clear, it extends not only to negotiations between a player and a Club of which he is not a member, but also to any "dealings" between them regarding employment. The prohibited dealings include both direct and indirect contacts.

a) *No Direct Contacts Without Written Consent*: There should be no direct contacts of any kind between a Club and players on another Club without the prior *written* consent of the current Club. Oral permission to contact another Club is *not* permitted. Written consent may be granted only if (i) the two Clubs have agreed on the terms under which an assignment of the player's contract would be made by one to the other and (ii) waivers are in effect with respect to any player(s) whose assignment would require them. If *written* consent is given, a copy of it together with the terms of the player transaction should be sent immediately by teletype by the consenting Club to this office and to its League Office. Such permissions must be limited to a period of no longer than 72 hours, by which time they will be deemed to have automatically expired. Also, please refrain from granting permissions during periods when the affected Clubs are scheduled to play each other. As stated above, the granting of *oral* permission by a Club to a player on its roster "to attempt to work out a deal with another Club" is a violation of Rule 3(g), as is any contact between such player and another Club pursuant to such oral permission.

b) *Indirect Contacts*: The indirect contacts which are prohibited include (i) public comments by a Club indicating an interest or desire in acquiring the contract of a player on another Club; (ii) public comments by a player indicating an interest or desire to contract with another Club; (iii) contacts between a Club and the agent of a player on another Club; and (iv) contacts between such Clubs and players through any other third-party intermediary.

c) (i) *Player Agents*: As above indicated, all players under contract or reservation to a Club—including potential Re-Entry Draft players—are prohibited from contacting other Clubs either directly or through their agents. This means that each player who has authorized an agent to represent him is responsible for controlling the activities of the agent to assure that they conform to the requirements of this bulletin. In cases where tampering violations are established involving the activities of agents, action may be taken against Clubs, Club personnel, players and/or agents. *Remedies against agents may include disqualification from future player representation.*

To acquaint player agents with tampering provisions, copies of this bulletin are being distributed to all agents known to this office.

(ii) *Written Authorization of Agents*: The provisions of this office's Notice No. 41 dated October 16, 1980 are still in effect. This means, among other things, that before any player can be represented in contract negotiations by an agent, such player must first have executed and delivered to his Club the standard form of letter of authorization, copies of which the Club is required to file with the Players' Association, the Player Relations Committee, the appropriate League Office and this office. Notice No. 41 will be updated and reissued later this summer, but additional copies of that Notice—which remains in full force and effect in the meantime—are available upon request from this office.

I would also remind all recipients of this bulletin that anyone having knowledge that a violation of the above prohibitions has or may have occurred should communicate the pertinent facts to this office immediately. I continue to regard enforcement of this rule as most important and will not hesitate to impose serious penalties for its violation. I request all concerned to govern themselves accordingly. Your cooperation is appreciated.

Sincerely yours,

Bowie Kuhn

PLAYER'S AUTHORIZATION FORM

DATE: _____

TO: _____
(CLUB)
_____
(Address)

Dear _____

This will advise effective as of this date I have authorized

_____
(Agent)
_____
(Firm)
_____
(Address)
_____
(Telephone)

to act as my exclusive representative for the purpose of negotiating for inclusion in a Uniform Player's Contract the salary and Special Covenants, if any, which actually or potentially provide additional benefits to me as defined by the Basic Agreement and the interpretations thereof, subject to my right to approve the results of such negotiations through execution by me of such contract.

This authorization will remain in effect until the aforementioned Uniform Player's Contract is executed, or until the authorization is revoked by me in writing, whichever is the earlier.

_____
(Player's Signature)
_____
(Print Name of Player)
_____
(Social Security Number)

cc Commissioner
    League President
    Players Association
    Player Relations Committee

F: California Statute Regulating Agents

California is the first state to regulate sports agents. After California enacted its law in the fall of 1981, other state legislatures, including that of New York, began to consider similar legislation. The California law, which was strongly supported by the NFL Players Association, requires all agents for team sports athletes doing business in California (except California lawyers acting as legal counsel) to register annually, pay a license fee, and deposit a $10,000 surety bond. Regulations to implement the law were adopted in the fall of 1982 and the state labor commission intends to aggressively enforce the law. The California scheme is discussed in Question 19, "Who regulates agents?" The text of the California statute follows.

The people of the State of California do enact as follows:

SECTION 1. Chapter 1 (commencing with Section 1500) is added to Part 6 of Division 2 of the Labor Code, to read:

CHAPTER 1. ATHLETE AGENCIES
Article 1. Definitions

1500. The following definitions shall govern the construction of this chapter:

(a) "Person" means any individual, company, corporation, association, partnership, or their agents or employees.

(b) "Athlete agency" means any person who, as an independent contractor, directly or indirectly, recruits or solitics any person to enter into any agency contract or professional sport services contract, or for a fee procures, offers, promises, or attempts to obtain employment for any person with a professional sport team.

"Athlete agency" does not include any employee of a professional sport team, and does not include any member of the State Bar of California when acting as legal counsel for any person.

(c) "Agency contract" means any contract or agreement pursuant to which a person authorizes or empowers an athlete agency to negotiate or solicit on behalf of such person with one or more professional sport teams for the employment of such person by one or more professional sport teams.

(d) "Professional sport services contract" means any contract or agreement pursuant to which a person is employed or agrees to render services as a participant or player on a professional sport team.

Article 2. Registration

1510. No person shall engage in or carry on the occupation of an athlete agency without first registering with the Labor Commissioner.

1511. A written application for registration shall be made to the Labor Commissioner in the form prescribed by him or her and shall state all of the following:

(a) The name and address of the applicant.

(b) The street and number of the building or place where the business of the athlete agency is to be conducted.

(c) The business or occupation engaged in by the applicant for at least two years immediately preceding the date of application.

(d) If the applicant is other than a corporation, the names and addresses of all persons, except bona fide employees on stated salaries, financially interested, either as partners, associates, or profit sharers, in the operation of the athlete agency in question, together with the amount of their respective interests.

If the applicant is a corporation, the corporate name, the names, residential addresses, and telephone numbers of all officers of the corporation, the names of all persons exercising managing responsibility in the applicant or registrant's office, and the names and addresses of all persons having a financial interest of 10 percent or more in the business and the percentage of financial interest owned by such persons.

The application must be accompanied by affidavits of at least two reputable residents, who have known or been associated with the applicant for two years, of the city or county in which the business of the athlete agency is to be conducted that the applicant is a person of good moral character or, in the case of a corporation, has a reputation for fair dealing.

1512. Upon receipt of an application for a registration, the Labor Commissioner may cause an investigation to be made as to the character and responsibility of the applicant and of the premises designated in such application as the place in which it is proposed to conduct the business of the athlete agency.

1513. The commissioner, upon proper notice and hearing, may refuse to grant a license. The proceedings shall be conducted in accordance with Chapter 5 (commencing at Section 11500) of Part 1 of Division 3 of Title 2 of the Government Code, and the commissioner shall have all the power granted therein.

1514. No registration shall be granted to conduct the business of an athlete agency to a person whose registration has been revoked within three years from the date of application.

1515. The registration when first issued shall run to the next birthday of the applicant, and each license shall then be renewed within the 30 days preceding the licensee's birthday and shall run from birthday to birthday. In case the applicant is a partnership, such license shall be renewed within the 30 days preceding the birthday of the oldest partner. If the applicant is a corporation, such license shall be renewed within the 30 days preceding the anniversary of the date the corporation was lawfully formed. Renewal shall require the filing of an application for renewal, a renewal bond, and the payment of the annual license fee, but the Labor Commissioner may demand that a new application or new bond be submitted.

If the applicant or licensee desires, in addition, a branch office license, he shall file an application in accordance with the provisions of this section as heretofore set forth.

1516. All applications for renewal shall state the names and addresses of all persons, except bona fide employees on stated salaries, financially interested either as partners, associates, or profit sharers, in the operation of the business of the athlete agency.

1517. (a) A filing fee shall be paid to the Labor Commissioner at the time the application for issuance of an athlete agency license is filed.

(b) In addition to the filing fee required for application for issuance of an athlete agency license, every athlete agency shall pay to the Labor Commissioner annually at the time a license is issued or renewed, a license fee and a fee for each branch office maintained by the athlete agency in this state.

(c) A filing fee shall also be paid to the Labor Commissioner at the time application for consent to the transfer or assignment of an athlete agency registration is made but no fee shall be required upon the assignment or transfer of a registration.

The location of an athlete agency shall not be changed without the written consent of the Labor Commission.

1518. The Labor Commissioner shall set the fees required by Section 1517 in the amount necessary to generate sufficient revenue to cover the costs of administration and enforcement of this chapter.

1519. An athlete agency shall also deposit with the Labor Commissioner, prior to the issuance of renewal of a registration, a surety bond in the penal sum of ten thousand dollars ($10,000).

1520. Such surety bonds shall be payable to the people of the State of California, and shall be conditioned that the person applying for the registration will comply with this chapter and will pay all sums due any individual or group of individuals when such person or his representative or agent has received such sums, and will pay all damages occasioned to any person by reason of misstatement, misrepresentation, fraud, deceit, or any unlawful acts or omissions of the registered athlete agency, or its agents or employees, while acting within the scope of their employment.

1521. If any registrant fails to file a new bond with the Labor Commissioner within 30 days after notice of cancellation by the surety of the bond required under Section 1519, the registration issued to the principal under the bond is suspended until such time as a new surety bond is filed. A person whose registration is suspended pursuant to this section shall not carry on the business of an athlete agency during the period of such suspension.

1522. All moneys collected for licenses and all fines collected for violations of the provisions of this chapter shall be paid into the State Treasury and credited to the General Fund.

1523. Each registration shall contain all of the following:

(a) The name of the registrant.

(b) A designation of the city, street, and number of the place in which the registrant is authorized to carry on the business of an athlete agency.

(c) The number and date of issuance of the registration.

1524. No registration shall protect any other than the person to whom it is issued nor any places other than those designated in the registration. No registration shall be transferred or assigned to any person unless written consent is obtained from the Labor Commissioner.

1525. The Labor Commissioner may issue to a person eligible therefor a certificate of convenience to conduct the business of an athlete agency where the person registered to conduct the athlete agency business has died, or has been declared incompetent by the judgment of a court of competent jurisdiction, or has had a conservator appointed for his estate by a court of competent jurisdiction. Such a certificate of convenience may be denominated an estate certificate of convenience.

1526. To be eligible for a certificate of convenience, a person shall be any one of the following:

(a) The executor or administrator of the estate of a deceased person registered to conduct the business of an athlete agency.

(b) If no executor or administrator has been appointed, the surviving spouse or heir otherwise entitled to conduct the business of such deceased registrant.

(c) The guardian of the estate of an incompetent person registered as an athlete agency, or the conservator appointed for the conservation of the estate of a person registered to conduct the business of an athlete agency.

Such estate certificate of convenience shall continue in force for a period of not to exceed 90 days, and shall be renewable for such period as the Labor Commissioner may deem appropriate, pending the disposal of the athlete agency registration or the procurement of a new registration under the provisions of this chapter.

1527. The Labor Commissioner may revoke or suspend any registration when any one of the following is shown:

(a) The registrant or his agent has violated or failed to comply with any of the provisions of this chapter.

(b) The registrant has ceased to be of good moral character.

(c) The conditions under which the registration was issued have changed or no longer exist.

1528. Before revoking or suspending any registration, the Labor Commissioner shall afford the holder of such registration an opportunity to be heard in person or by counsel. The proceedings shall be conducted in accordance with

Chapter 5 (commencing at Section 11500) of Part 1 of Division 3 of Title 2 of the Government Code, and the commissioner shall have all the powers granted therein.

Article 3. Operation and Management

1530. Every athlete agency shall submit to the Labor Commissioner a form or forms of contract to be utilized by such agency in entering into written contracts with persons for the employment of the services of the agency by such persons, and secure the approval of the Labor Commissioner thereof. Such approval shall not be withheld as to any proposed form of contract unless such proposed form of contract is unfair, unjust, and oppressive to the person. Each such form of contract, except under the conditions specified in Section 1544, shall contain an agreement by the agency to refer any controversy between the person and the agency relating to the terms of the contract to the Labor Commissioner for adjustment. There shall be printed on the face of the contract in prominent type the following: "This athlete agency is registered with the Labor Commissioner of the State of California. Registration does not imply approval by the Labor Commissioner of the terms and conditions of this contract or the competence of the athlete agency."

1503.5. The contract shall contain in close proximity to the signature of the athlete a notice in at least 10-point type stating that the athlete may jeopardize his or her standing as an amateur athlete by entering into the contract.

1531. Every person engaged in the occupation of an athlete agency shall file with the Labor Commissioner a schedule of fees to be charged and collected in the conduct of such occupation. Changes in the schedule may be made from time to time, but no change shall become effective until seven days after the date of filing thereof with the Labor Commissioner.

1532. Every athlete agency shall keep records approved by the Labor Commissioner, in which shall be entered all of the following:

(a) The name and address of each person employing the athlete agency.

(b) The amount of fee received from such person.

(c) Other information which the Labor Commissioner requires.

No agency, its agent or employees, shall make any false entry in any such records.

1533. All books, records, and other papers kept pursuant to this chapter by any athlete agency shall be open at all reasonable hours to the inspection of the Labor Commissioner and his agents. Every agency shall furnish to the Labor Commissioner upon request a true copy of such books, records, and papers or any portion thereof, and shall make such reports as the Labor Commissioner prescribes.

1534. The Labor Commissioner may, in accordance with the provisions of Chapter 3.5 (commencing at Section 11340) of Part 1 of Division 3 of Title 2 of the Government Code, adopt, amend, and repeal such rules and regulations as are reasonably necessary for the purpose of enforcing and administering this chapter and as are not inconsistent with this chapter.

1535. No registrant shall sell, transfer, or give away any interest in or the right to participate in the profits of the agency without the written consent of the Labor Commissioner. A violation of this section shall constitute a misdemeanor, and shall be punishable by a fine of not less than one hundred dollars ($100) nor more than five hundred dollars ($500), or imprisonment for not more than 60 days, or both.

1536. No athlete agency shall knowingly issue a contract containing any term or condition which, if complied with, would be in violation of law, or attempt to fill an order for help to be employed in violation of law.

1537. No athlete agency shall publish or cause to be published any false, fraudulent, or misleading information, representation, notice, or advertisement. All advertisements of an agency by means of cards, circulars, or signs, and in newspapers and other publications, and all letterheads, receipts, and blanks shall be printed and contain the registered name and address of the agency and the words "athlete agency." No athlete agency shall give any false information or make any false promises or representations concerning any employment to any person.

1538. No athlete agency shall knowingly secure employment for persons in any place where a strike, lockout, or other labor trouble exists, without notifying the person of such conditions.

1539. No athlete agency shall divide fees with an employer, an agent, or other employee of an employer.

1540. In the event that an athlete agency shall collect from a person a fee or expenses for obtaining employment, and the person shall fail to procure such employment, or the person shall fail to be paid for such employment, the agency shall, upon demand therefor, repay to the person the fee and expenses so collected. Unless repayment thereof is made within 48 hours after demand therefor, the agency shall pay to the person an additional sum equal to the amount of the fee.

1541. All actions brought in any court against any registrant may be brought in the name of the person damaged upon the bond deposited with the state by the registrant, and may be transferred and assigned as other claims for damages. The amount of damages claimed by plaintiff, and not the penalty named in the bond, determines the jurisdiction of the court in which the action is brought.

1542. When a registrant has departed from the state with intent to defraud creditors or to avoid service of summons in an action brought under this chapter, service shall be made upon the surety as prescribed in the Code of Civil Procedure. A copy of the summons shall be mailed to the registrant at the last known post office address of his residence and also at the place where the business of the athlete agency was conducted as shown by the records of the Labor Commissioner. Service is complete as to such registrant, after mailing, at the expiration of the time prescribed by the Code of Civil Procedure for service of summons in the particular court in which suit is brought.

1543. In cases of controversy arising under this chapter the parties involved shall refer the matters in dispute to the Labor Commissioner, who shall hear and determine the same, subject to an appeal within 10 days after determination, to the superior court where the same shall be heard de novo. To stay any award for money, the party aggrieved shall execute a bond approved by the superior court in a sum not exceeding twice the amount of the judgment. In all other cases the bond shall be in a sum of not less than ten thousand dollars ($10,000) and approved by the superior court.

The Labor Commissioner may certify without a hearing that there is no controversy within the meaning of this section if he has by investigation established that there is no dispute as to the amount of the fee due. Service of such certification shall be made upon all parties concerned by registered or certified mail with return receipt requested and such certification shall become conclusive 10 days after the date of mailing if no objection has been filed with the Labor Commissioner during that period.

1544. Notwithstanding Section 1543, a provision in a contract providing for the decision by arbitration of any controversy under the contract or as to its existence, validity, construction, performance, nonperformance, breach, operation, continuance, or termination, shall be valid:

(a) If the provision is contained in a contract between an athlete agency and a person for whom the agency under the contract undertakes to endeavor to secure employment,

(b) If the provision is inserted in the contract pursuant to any rule, regulation, or contract of a bona fide labor union regulating the relations of its members to an agency,

(c) If the contract provides for reasonable notice to the Labor Commissioner of the time and place of all arbitration hearings, and

(d) If the contract provides that the Labor Commissioner or his authorized representative has the right to attend all arbitration hearings.

Except as otherwise provided in this section, any such arbitration shall be governed by the provisions of Title 9 (commencing with Section 1280) of Part 3 of the Code of Civil Procedure.

If there is such an arbitration provision in such a contract, the contract need not provide that the agency agrees to refer any controversy between the person and the agency regarding the terms of the contract to the Labor Commissioner for adjustment, and Section 1543 shall not apply to controversies pertaining to the contract.

A provision in a contract providing for the decision by arbitration of any controversy arising under this chapter which does not meet the requirements of this section is not made valid by Section 1281 of the Code of Civil Procedure.

1545. (a) An athlete agency shall, prior to communicating with or contacting in any manner any student concerning an agency contract or a professional sport services contract, file with the secondary or postsecondary educational institution at which the student is enrolled a copy of the registration certificate of the athlete agency.

(b) An athlete agency shall file a copy of each agency contract made with any student, with the secondary or postsecondary educational institution at which the student is enrolled, within five days after such contract is signed by the student party thereto.

(c) Filing of the copies required by subdivisions (a) and (b) shall be made with the president or chief administrative officer of the secondary or postsecondary educational institution, or the secretary of such officer, or by registered or certified mail, return receipt requested, directed to such officer.

1546. Any agency contract which is negotiated by any agency who has failed to comply with Section 1510 or 1545 is void and unenforceable.

1547. Any person, or agent or officer thereof, who violates any provision of this chapter is guilty of a misdemeanor, punishable by a fine of not less than one thousand dollars ($1,000) or imprisonment for a period of not more than 60 days, or both.

G: Directory

Players' Associations

Baseball

Major League Baseball Players Association
1370 Avenue of the Americas
New York, NY 10019
(212) 581-8484

Basketball

National Basketball Players Association
15 Columbus Circle
New York, NY 10023
(212) 541-7118

Football

Canadian Football League Players Association
1300 Dewdney Avenue
Regina, Saskatchewan
(306) 569-0167

National Football League Players Association
1300 Connecticut Avenue, N.W.
Suite 407
Washington, D.C. 20036
(202) 463-2200

Golf

PGA Tour
100 Nina Court
Ponte Vedra Beach, FL 32082
(904) 285-3700
Commissioner: Deane Beman

LPGA
1250 Shoreline Drive
Sugar Land, TX 77478
(713) 980-5742
Commissioner: John Laupheimer

Hockey

National Hockey League Players' Association
The Thompson Building
65 Queen Street, N.W.
Toronto, Canada M5H 2M5
(416) 868-6574

Soccer

Major Indoor Soccer League Players Association
North American Soccer League Players Association
1300 Connecticut Avenue, N.W.
Suite 407
Washington, D.C. 20036
(202) 463-2200

Tennis

Association of Tennis Professionals
60 E. 42nd Street
Suite 1812
New York, NY 10165
(212) 370-0330
Executive Director: Butch Buchholz, Jr.

Women's Tennis Association
1604 Union Street
San Francisco, CA 94123
(415) 673-2018
Executive Director:
 Jerry Diamond

Football

Canadian Football League
Suite 1800
908-11 King Street W.
Toronto, Ontario M5H 1A3
(416) 366-8591

National Football League
410 Park Avenue
New York, NY 10022
(212) 758-1500

United States Football League
52 Vanderbilt Avenue, 4th Floor
New York, NY 10017
(212) 682-6363

Leagues

Baseball

Major League Baseball
Office of the Commissioner
15 W. 51st Street
New York, NY 10019
(212) 586-7400

(Minor League Baseball)
National Association of Professional
 Baseball Leagues
201 Bayshore Drive S.E.
P.O. Box A
St. Petersburg, FL 33731
(813) 822-6937

Basketball

National Basketball Association
Olympic Tower
645 Fifth Avenue
New York, NY 10022
(212) 826-7000

Hockey

National Hockey League
960 Sun Life Building
Montreal, Canada H3B 2W2
(514) 871-9220

or

National Hockey League
1221 Avenue of the Americas
New York, NY 10020
(212) 398-1100

Soccer

Major Indoor Soccer League
1 Bala Cynwd Plaza
Bala Cynwd, PA 19004
(215) 667-8020

North American Soccer League
1133 Avenue of the Americas
New York, NY 10036
(212) 575-0066

NCAA

National Collegiate Athletic
   Association
P.O. Box 1906
Mission, KS 66201
(913) 384-3220

Lawyers and Agents Organizations

American Bar Association
Forum Committee on the
   Entertainment and Sports
   Industries
1155 East 60th Street
Chicago, IL 60637
(312) 947-3853

Association of Representatives of
   Professional Athletes
9111 South LaCienega Blvd.
Suite 205
Inglewood, CA 90301
(213) 670-1915

Sports Lawyers Association
444 N. Michigan Avenue
Suite 2300
Chicago, IL 60611
(312) 527-4000

Sources

This book is based on information compiled from June 1977 to September 1982. Interviews and newspaper and magazine articles formed the basis for the original paper prepared for the Harvard Law School. This expanded version evolved from comments on that manuscript, further research and discussion about the subject, and reflection on changes in the nature of athlete-agent problems and issues.

Much of the expanded material is attributable to discussions at three meetings: a seminar sponsored by Indiana University Law School on Amateur Sports and the Law, August 20–22, 1981, in Indianapolis; the Association of Representatives of Professional Athletes annual meeting on October 18, 1981, in Baltimore; and the American Bar Association Forum Committee on the Entertainment and Sports Industries, Sports Division Seminar on March 26–27, 1982, in Houston. The book also benefitted from access to correspondence between the Collegiate Commissioners Association and college coaches, college athletic administrators, and professional league and players' associations staff concerning agent problems. Discussions at meetings of the NCAA Professional Sports Liaison Committee in February and May 1982, attended by representatives of the NFL, the NBA, and Major League Baseball also provided useful information.

The following persons participated in interviews or commented on drafts of the book or both: Martin Blackman, Michael Burke, C. Kent Carlson, William Carpenter, John Claiborne, Wayne Duke, Alan Eagleson, Bob Epstein, Donald Fehr, Joseph Garagiola, Jr., Russell Granik, Richard Greenberg, Michael Halstead, Armond Hill, Arthur Kaminsky, Bill Madden, Tom McMillan, Richard Moss, James Quinn, Jeff Ruland (via "Sports Talk," WTOP Radio, Washington, D.C.), Stephen Schneider, Lloyd Shefsky, Mark Softy, George Taliaferro, John Thompson (Seattle Seahawks), Bob Tufts, Gary Walters, William Westin, and Bob Woolf. Several other persons who also participated in similar fashion are listed in the Preface. Major League Baseball, the NASL, the NBA, and the NHL league offices and the baseball, basketball, football, and soccer players' associations supplied information, particularly in regard to player salaries, uniform contracts, and draft processes.

The sources are listed chronologically (beginning with the most recent articles and working back) and are presented in several topical divisions: general articles about agents, articles about particular agents, articles about particular athletes, articles about contract issues, and articles about amateurism. Books and congressional documents are listed following the newspaper and periodical articles.

Newspaper and Periodical Articles

General Articles about Agents
"Sports Representatives Sue Former Clients," Sports Lawyers Association Newsletter, Spring-Summer 1982, at 16.
Reilly, "The $ Peddlers: Athletes Fall Easy Prey to Shady Agents," *Denver Post*, 16 May 1982, at 8E.
Balzer, "Mysteries of the NFL Draft: Who's the Agent?" *The Sporting News*, 10 May 1982, at 43.
McDonough, "Agents' playoffs spell big payoffs," *Boston Sunday Globe*, 9 May 1982, at 76.
Kirshenbaum (ed.), "Sports Agents: Raising Ethical Questions that Run from A (Armas) to Z (Zadora)," *Sports Illustrated*, 12 April 1982, at 21.
Nightingale, "Are Agents Pack of Parasites?" *The Sporting News* (three-part series), 6, 13, and 20 February 1982.
Melvin, "Agents: Makers or takers? Sweet talk agents' calling card," *San Francisco Sunday Examiner & Chronicle*, 31 May 1981, at C-5.
Moore, "Agents: Anything but typical," *Oakland Tribune*, 2 March 1981, at D-5.
Chicago Tribune, 13 October 1980, section 4, at 10 (Midwest Edition).
Barnes, "Agent's Role Draws Fire," *Washington Post*, 10 August 1980, at D-1.
Kornheiser, "Sorkin Tells State Crime Unit Sports Agents Duped Clients," *The New York Times*, 2 February 1978, at 48.
Katz, "N.F.L. Players Organize a Group to List Agents," *The New York Times*, 15 January 1978, at V-10.
Ray, "Miller Raps Player-Agent Excesses," *The Sporting News*, 12 February 1977, at 33.
Lauck, "Agents in Sports: The Hidden Scandal," *Newsday* (four-part series), 23-27 January 1977.

Sources

Articles about Particular Agents
Gammons, "A Pressurized Vote for Rookie Ripken," *The Sporting News*, 20 September 1982, at 53.
Brubacker, "The No. 1 Headache for Last Year's No. 1 Pick," *Inside Sports*, April 1982, at 65.
Dreyfus and Eisenberg, "Seven of the Best," *Money*, April 1982, at 52.
Barnes, "Athletes' Lives and Livelihoods are ProServ's Stock and Trade," *Washington Post*, 19 July 1981, at D-14.
Moore, "Bunning likes being an agent," *Oakland Tribune*, 2 March 1981, at D-5.
Johnson, "Al Gave It His All," *Sports Illustrated*, 5 January 1981, at 26.
Goldenberg, "Hockey's Superagent," *The New York Times*, 31 August 1980, at 7.
Ruby, "What Agents Do for Clients," *Inside Sports*, 30 June 1980, at 106.
"Duval Files for Bankruptcy," *The New York Times*, 18 January 1978, at B-6.
"Slusher: The Agent Behind N.F.L. Players Who Stay Away," *The New York Times*, 23 October 1977, at 9.
Montgomery, "The Spectacular Rise and Ignoble Fall of Richard Sorkin, Pros' Agent," *The New York Times*, 9 October 1977, at V-1.
Weiner, "Erving's Manager Says Nets Reneged," *The New York Times*, 21 November 1976, at V-1.
Woolf, "His Ex-Manager Talks of Commitment," *The New York Times*, 21 November 1976, at V-1.

Articles about Particular Athletes
Raissman, "What Price Glory," *Inside Sports*, August 1982, at 42.
Gammons, "Alexander Deal May Cost George," *The Sporting News*, 17 April 1982, at 21.
Underwood, "Does Herschel Have Georgia on His Mind?" *Sports Illustrated*, 1 March 1982, at 22.
Goddard, "Cubs' Buckner: No Pay, No Play," *The Sporting News*, 30 January 1982, at 52.
Wright, "Sikma Has the Sonics Revved Up," *The Sporting News*, 23 January 1982, at 35.
Bodley, "Bowa Furious at Phils' Deceit," *The Sporting News*, 16 January 1982, at 46.
Doughty, "Mighty Sampson Returns," *The Sporting News*, 5 December 1981, at 11.
"Agents Firing Money Pitch," *The Sporting News*, 1 April 1978, at 40.

Lang, "Randle Calms Down, Joins Mets After Money Hassle," *The Sporting News*, 18 March 1978, at 52.
Collier, "Padres Convert a Contract Boner Into Lolich," *The Sporting News*, 18 February 1978, at 43.

Articles about Contract Issues
Axthelm, "They're Playing for Keeps," *Newsweek*, 20 September 1982, at 70.
Isle, "Twins See Youth Movement as Way to Bottle Lightning," *The Sporting News*, 13 March 1982, at 12.
Gammons, "Yaz Unique in High-Turnover Era," *The Sporting News*, 27 February 1982, at 41.
Boswell, "Baseball Strike's Reverse Effect: Player Salaries Continue to Rise," *Washington Post*, 14 February 1982, at D-1.
"Bonds Settles for $215,000," *The Sporting News*, 13 February 1982, at 46.
Conlin, "Salary Insanity Still Is Unchecked," *The Sporting News*, 13 February 1982, at 37.
Wigge, "Gretzky's Reward—$20 Million for 15 Years," *The Sporting News*, 6 February 1982, at 35.
Klein, "The Golden Age of Salaries," *Inside Sports*, August 1981, at 58, especially chart at 69.
Ray, "Cable Can Be A Boon Or A Pain To Sports," *The Sporting News*, 13 June 1981, at 14.
Baker, "Cable Sports: Whose Court Is This Ball In, Anyway?" *Cablevision*, 11 May 1981, at 38.
Young, "Young Ideas," *The Sporting News*, 18 March 1978, at 16.
Durso, "Big Problem Is Arising in Baseball: How Much Should a Superstar Get?" *The New York Times*, 5 March 1978, at V-1.
"Sports Enter the Labor Relations Arena," *Industrial and Labor Relations Report*, Fall 1977, at 21.

Articles about Amateurism
Ruxin, "Unsportsmanlike Conduct: The Student-Athlete, the NCAA, and Agents," *Journal of College & University Law*, 347 (1981).
Feinstein, "NBA and Undergraduates: An Anguished Relationship," *Washington Post*, 10 May 1981, at D-1.
Shannon, "Agent Should Be Part of Changing College Scene," *The New York Times*, 30 November 1980, at V-2.
Kornheiser, "Insurance for College Stars," *Washington Post*, 27 April 1980 at N-1.

Benagh, "Sports Insurance Business: A Billion Dollars in Policies," *The New York Times*, 7 April 1980, at C-12.
Horn, "Intercollegiate Athletics: Waning Amateurism and Rising Professionalism," *Journal of College & University Law*, 97 (1978).

Books

Berry and Wong. *The Sports Industries: Legal and Business Materials.* Mimeographed, 1980.
Gallner, Sheldon. *Pro Sports: The Contract Game.* New York: Charles Scribner's Sons, 1974.
NCAA. *1982-83 Manual of the National Collegiate Athletic Association.* Mission, Kansas: NCAA, 1982.
Woolf, Bob. *Behind Closed Doors.* New York: Antheneum, 1976.

Congressional Documents

NCAA Enforcement Program, Hearings Before the Subcommittee on Oversight and Investigation of the House Committee on Interstate and Foreign Commerce, 95th Cong., 2d Sess. (1978).
Enforcement Program of the National Collegiate Athletic Association, Report of Subcommittee on Oversight and Investigation of the House Committee on Interstate and Foreign Commerce, Comm. Print 95-69, 95th Cong., 2d Sess. (1977).
Inquiry into Professional Sports, Hearings Before the House Select Committee on Professional Sports, 94th Cong., 2d Sess. (1977).
Inquiry into Professional Sports, House Select Committee on Professional Sports, Final Report H.R. Rep. No 94-1786, 94th Cong., 2d Sess. (1977).